THE JACK THE RIPPER HANDBOOK

A READER'S COMPANION

ROSS

FOREWORD BY STEWART P. EVANS.

PUBLISHED ON BEHALF OF THE AUTHOR
BY
GREAT SCOT SERVICES.

Published Privately By The Author.

Printed in the UK by
Great Scot Services
Portland Business Centre
Irvine
Scotland KA12 8JE.

This book is dedicated to my wife, Susan, who encouraged and supported me all the way, even after years of listening to my ramblings on the case and visiting more bookshops than I care to remember.

CONTENTS.

ACKNOWLEDGEMENTS.

During my search for as much information as I could possibly find on the subject of the literature on the Whitechapel Murders I encountered many people who assisted me with my research. Some gave sound advice and others furnished me with information of which I was unaware.

To these people I owe many thanks indeed, and I would like to publically acknowledge:-

Andy Aliffe; Stephane Bourgoin; Ed Chick; Paul Daniel; Stewart Evans; Professor Christopher Frayling; Dave Froggatt; Robert Ives; Coral Kelly; Loretta Lay; Peter Riley; Stephen Ryder; Sabine Schnatz; Darren Sevket; Dixon Smith; John Smithkey III; Mel Steinfeld; Judith Stock; Lars Thomas; Eric Tromp; Dave Upton; Nick Warren and Camille Wolff.

A great deal of gratitude must also go to Margaret Gunn who performed a minor miracle in turning my handwritten work into an excellently produced manuscript, and the advice given was always appreciated.

My friend, Steven Grier, also provided me with a computer and without this I would have struggled greatly to obtain as much information as I have. I am extremely grateful.

A big thank you to Laura Clark for designing the front cover of this book.

THE WOMEN WHO DIED.

FOREWORD.

Ross Strachan has already established himself as something of an authority on obscure and rare literature related to 'Jack the Ripper'. His popular guide to the available literature, *Jack the Ripper: A Collector's Guide To The Many Books Published,* has become a must for all collectors of Ripper related titles. His knowledge is fuelled by his great enthusiasm to record every single Ripper related title and collectable he could find. Indeed, it would be fair to describe him as arguably the greatest authority in this area of the field. He has travelled far (including a visit to Stephane Bourgoin in Paris), and corresponded at great length in his quest to record all that is available. And I do not hesitate to state that if there is some elusive title that I am seeking to learn more about he is the first person I consult. If a book can be found, Ross will find it. He has already supplied me with more than one of the harder to find titles in my own collection.

This work is truly a readers', and a collectors', companion, but more than this, it is an invaluable reference tool for all those interested in the subject. He does not seek to replace other bibliographies, but rather presents his own work in his own inimitable style, and thus provides a work which contains some references you will find in no other bibliography. He also painstakingly lists all magazine references, foreign titles and collectables. Others will find the audio and music lists useful, and the reference sections of useful information and addresses is a must for all those wishing to expand their knowledge. The listing of all known foreign works is particularly valuable, and gives the book a truly international appeal. Ross highly recommends the 'Alexander Kelly' bibliography, and so would I, but do not dispense with that volume, merely place this one alongside it on your bookshelf.

As an old friend of Ross I am very pleased, and honoured, to be allowed to comment on his work in this way. It is for all the best reasons that Ross's name is already well known to all Ripper writers, collectors and enthusiasts. He appeared in Channel 4's

Collector's Lot and was an immediate hit with all who saw the transmission. Although his first work was very good, it has now matured and improved over the years, as will be seen by all who read the present volume. No Ripper writer, historian, collector or enthusiast should be without a copy of Ross Strachan's *Jack the Ripper Handbook And Reader's Companion;* it is now an essential work of reference.

Stewart P Evans
Isleham, Cambs.
September 1999.

INTRODUCTION.

The Whitechapel Murders of 1888, or the Jack the Ripper Murders as they are better known, still capture the imagination of people worldwide.

Since these horrendous crimes were committed the world has advanced so much that it is inconceivable to imagine life back in those black days. Today things we take for granted such as electricity, motor cars, air travel, computers, even proper health care and sanitation would have been unimaginable to anyone residing in the East End of London during 1888.

However, in this modern age the crimes of Jack the Ripper have not been forgotten - if anything they are of more interest to us now than they have ever been.

Since these foul murders were committed there has been a steady flow of books, magazines, comics, films, television shows etc. dedicated to the subject of Jack the Ripper. Most have attempted to understand the crimes, find a motive and, of course, try to unmask the killer. We have learned much from all the literature but I'm afraid to say that we are no nearer to putting a name to Jack the Ripper and, in all probability, the killer's identity will forever remain a mystery. If the Police at the time could not solve the case, how can we expect to do so all these years later?

It is not only in Britain that the murders prove to be of interest. The crimes have been written about in many countries and languages, with Ripper enthusiasts being found in all the far flung corners of the globe.

Since the Ripper committed his crimes there have been more vicious, more sickening and more inhuman killers walking our streets. Serial killers such as Ted Bundy, Dennis Nilsen and Peter Sutcliffe, a.k.a. The Yorkshire Ripper; child murderers including Fred and Rose West and even cannibal killers where people such as Jeffrey Dahmer murdered and ate parts of his victims - but still Jack the Ripper remains the name on our lips when we discuss horrific crimes and cases of mass murder.

Why this fascination for a series of murders committed all those years ago?

Possibly the fact that the crimes were never solved and that no-one has been brought to justice, coupled with the conspiracy theories which surround the case, keep it in the public eye and, of course, the name given to the killer - JACK THE RIPPER - is not easily forgotten. Even today experts cannot agree on many points regarding the murders. For years the general feeling was that five victims fell foul of the Ripper, however today we cannot be sure of this although I think it is fair to say that between three and six women were murdered by the Ripper during the Autumn of 1888.

The Ripper killings as entertainment have now become an accepted part of society. There is a healthy demand each year for new books on the case and today the amount of novels, short stories, poems and even computer games far outweigh the number of factual accounts published. Most of the fictional works manage to achieve something the so called factual books can't - they put a name to Jack the Ripper.

What is easily forgotten is the fact that the victims were real people with real lives which were cruelly cut short by the work of a crazed killer.

The object of this book is neither to take a look at the murders in detail nor to attempt to solve the case with a new theory. We are also not concerned with the vast amount of suspects named by authors and researchers during the past 110 or so years. What this work does is closely examine the many books, both factual and fictional, published on the subject of Jack the Ripper as well as all other related material including comic books, magazines, fanzines etc., from all around the world.

We will look at the many different editions available including foreign language works dedicated to the case. The collectable side of Jack the Ripper is discussed where the many ephemeral items such as records, movie posters and board games exist and are well worth tracking down.

Whether you are a budding Ripperologist, merely an enthusiast or a hardened collector of Ripper material - I'm sure that this book will have something to offer.

Over the next 100 years the amount of material published will, I'm sure, continue to flourish, although we must never forget the fact that eleven women were murdered in the East End between 3rd April 1888 and 13th February 1891, with no-one ever brought to justice. Maybe they were not all victims of Jack the Ripper, but they all deserved a better fate than they received.

The fact that their deaths brought the desperate conditions in the East End to the public eye is the only positive aspect to emerge from the killings.

<u>Ross Strachan.</u>
<u>October 1999.</u>

CHAPTER ONE

Relevant and Collectable Titles
on London and the East End.

Over the years thousands of books have been published dedicated to one of the greatest cities on Earth, London. The importance and cultural aspects of London have been studied in great detail; however, what interests us most is Victorian London and it's people, especially the East End where the Jack the Ripper murders occurred. Many excellent books exist which paint a picture of daily life and just how hard it could be for most people. When we can understand the squalor and poverty which had to be endured, maybe then we can comprehend the reality that in Whitechapel alone in 1888 approximately sixty two brothels existed and that as many as twelve hundred prostitutes plied their trade. For most of these women it was their only source of income.

In order to familiarise ourselves with the East End of London during the Ripper's reign of terror the following titles are recommended.

Some of the better factual studies written about the crimes also provide an insight into the conditions and harshness of the East End.

"The Complete Jack the Ripper" by Donald Rumbelow is one such example. Before the author takes us through the facts surrounding the first murder we have already had a detailed look at the area and it's inhabitants and are now well educated regarding the world in which the Ripper and his victims lived and worked.

Recommended Reading

| BESANT | *East London* | Chatto and Windass, London, 1901.
Century, New York, USA, 1901. |

LONDON Jack   *The People of the Abyss*

    MacMillan, London, 1903.
    MacMillan, New York, USA, 1903.
    Archer House, New York, USA 1963.
    Journeyman Press, London, P/B,
    1977 and 1992.
    Pluto Press, London, H/B and P/B,
    1998.

CHESNEY   *The Victorian Underworld.*
Kellow

    Maurice Temple Smith, London, 1970.
    Readers Union Group, Book Club,
    1970.
    Pelican, London, P/B, 1972.
    Penguin, London, P/B, 1991.

Retitled
The Anti Society: An Account of the Victorian
Underworld.

    Gambit, Boston, USA, 1970.

BERMANT   *Point of Arrival: A Study of London's East End.*
Chaim

    Eyre Methuen, London, 1975.

Retitled
London's East End: Point of Arrival.

    MacMillan, New York, USA, 1976.

FISHMAN   *The Streets of East London.*
William

    Duckworth, London, 1979.
    Reprinted Duckworth, London,
    P/B, 1980, '81, '83, '85, '87, '89, '92.

JONES Steve	*London: The Sinister Side.*
	Tragical History Tours Publications, Kent, 1986.
	Reprinted in P/B, Wicked Publications Nottingham, 1987 to 1995.

FISHMAN William   *East End 1888*   Duckworth, London, 1988.
Temple University Press, Philadelphia USA, 1988.

PALMER Ian   *The East End: Four Centuries of London.*
John Murray, London, 1989.

DAVIES Andrew   *The East End Nobody Knows*
Macmillan, London, 1990.

FARSON Daniel   *Limehouse Days:*
A Personal Experience of the East End.
Michael Joseph, London, 1991.

PHILPOTTS Robert   *On Foot In The East End (Volume 1)*
Blackwater Books, London, 1995, P/B.

THOMAS Donald   *The Victorian Underworld*
John Murray, London, 1997.

SAMUEL Raphael   *East End Underworld:*
Chapters in the Life of Arthur Harding.
Routledge & Kegan Paul, London, 1997

RAMSEY Winston G   *"The East End: Then and Now"*
Battle of Britain Prints International, London, 1997.

CHAPTER TWO
Factual Works Dedicated to Jack the Ripper.

PURKESS G   *The Whitechapel Murders: or*
               The Mysteries of The East End.
                         G.   Purkess, The Strand, London 1888
               Reprinted by Ripper researcher and historian Andy Aliffe
               in 1996.

               This was the first ever account of the Ripper killings
               and, incredibly, published before the murder of the
               final victim - Mary Kelly.
               Advertised in 1888 as a thrilling romance story!

ANON   *Jack the Ripper at Work Again:*
               Another terrible murder and mutilation in Whitechapel.
                         9th November London 1888.

               No more than a four page broadsheet giving details
               of the murder of Mary Kelly.

ANON   *The Whitechapel Atrocities: Arrest of a Newspaper*
               Reporter.
                         Woodford Fawcett & Co., Dorset Works,
                         Salisbury Square, London, UK, 1888.
                         Booklet. (Publishers price one penny).

               A facsimile edition was issued by Ripper researcher and
               historian, Andy Aliffe, in 1999.

FOX KYLE
Richard

The History of The Whitechapel Murders:
A full and authentic narrative of the above murders
with sketches.

>> Franklin Square, New York, USA,
>> 1888.

Reprinted by The Ripperological Preservation Society,
Paramus, New Jersey, USA in 1997.

HUDSON
Samuel E

Leather Apron: or The Horrors of Whitechapel,
London 1888.

>> Town Printing House, Chestnut Street,
>> Philadelphia, USA, 1888.

Reprinted by The Ripperological Preservation Society,
Paramus, New Jersey, USA in 1997

ANON

Chronicles of Crime and Criminals:
Whitechapel Murders by the Infamous Jack the Ripper.

>> Beaver Publishing Company, Toronto,
>> Canada,1895. No. 1.

Reprinted by The Ripperological Preservation Society,
Paramus, New Jersey, USA, 1997.

Draws heavily from the Richard Kyle Fox work.

HAYNE W.J.

Jack the Ripper: or The Crimes of London.

>> Utility Book and Novel Company,
>> Chicago, USA, 1889.

**This 66 page work was stolen from the Library of
Congress, New York, USA, sometime between 1889
and 1906.**

ANON

Jack Lo Squartotore.

>> Di Donne, Venice, Italy, 1889.

A 'penny dreadful' detailing the murders.

ANON   *The Latest Atrocities of Jack the Ripper.*
            Stuttgart, Germany, 1889.

ANON   *Hvem Ar Jack Uppskararen?*
          Berattelse Om Den Fasawackande
          Qwinnornord, Som Under Loppet Af Trenne
          Ar Blifwit Begangna I Stadsdelen Whiteschapel
          I Engelska Hufwudstaden London.
            Utgivningstar, Kalmar, Sweden, 1889
            (16 pages)

          Translates - Who Was Jack the Ripper? An examination
          of the woman murders committed over thirty years in
          Whitechapel, London.

MENARD Peter   *Certain Connections or Affinities with Jack the*
          Ripper.
            Nimmo, Edinburgh, Scotland, 1903.

MUUSMANN Carl *Hvem Var Jack the Ripper?*
            Kriminal-Bibliotheket, Hermann
            Petersen, Denmark, 1908.

          A facsimile edition released in 1999 by Ripper
          enthusiast Adam Wood of London, which was limited
          to 100 copies only, also earned an English language trans-
          lation of this very scarce work. A number of original cop-
          ies are still known to exist. A copy is held in the Royal
          Danish Library in Copenhagen. In the UK Ripper au-
          thor and expert Donald Rumbelow owns a copy of this
          very scarce work. In the book the Ripper is named as
          Alios Szemeredy.

ROBINSON Tom	*The Whitechapel Horrors - Being an Authentic Account of The Jack the Ripper Murders.*
	Daisy Bank Publishing, Manchester, England.
	Not dated (circa 1920's).

A pulp paperback which is now rare. A facsimile edition was produced in 1995 by Ripper researcher and historian Andy Aliffe.

MATTERS Leonard	*The Mystery of Jack the Ripper: The World's Greatest Crime Problem.*
	1^{stt} Published - Hutchinson and Co. Ltd., London 1928, H/B.

Red boards with gold lettering. With 10 illustrations and 5 diagrams. Copies are very hard to obtain. A second and third impression were produced in 1928 with blue boards and black lettering, although the same yellow and black dustjacket was issued. Re-printed - W.H. Allen and Co. Ltd., London 1948, in H/B with a new dustjacket. Copies were produced with both red and green boards.

**The book itself had a new introduction written by Matters in June 1948 although the contents were the same as the 1928 edition, however, it had fewer illustrations. It was described as the first cheap edition of the best book ever written on the world's greatest crime mystery. A paperback was also issued in 1948 by Pinnacle Books, for W.H. Allen. It was part of their Real Life Crime Stories Series (No. 5) and had a rather attractive cover.
Costing 2d at the time, copies are now difficult to obtain. Two other paperback copies of Matters exist. In 1960 Pedigree Books of London published his work with the sub-heading 'The Sensational Solution of the World's Greatest Crime Mystery'.**

This edition is scarce and much sought after. Probably
the most common edition is the 1964 P/B by Arrow
Books, London (No. 771). The cover shows a bloody
knife lying on a cobbled street.
Matters names a Doctor Stanley as the culprit who died
in Buenos Aires, Argentina. This rather far-fetched
theory sees Stanley avenging his son's death by murdering the prostitutes of Whitechapel.

DORSENNE Jean   *Jack l'Eventreur - Scenes Vecues.*
                                      Les Editions de France, France, 1935,
                                      P/B.

A now scarce factual account of the Ripper murders
which collectors will have great difficulty in obtaining.
An English language translation was published by
Cappella Archive Limited Editions, UK, in 1999 in hard
back complete with dustjacket. It was translated by
Molly Whittington-Egan, wife of Ripper author Richard,
who has written an introduction to this new edition.

NEIL Charles   *World's Greatest Mysteries - 'Jack the Ripper'*
(Editor)   *and 'Life in Atmospheria'*
                                      Charles Neil Publishing, Victoria,
                                      Australia.
                                      Illustrated. No date (circa 1936) P/B.

A facsimile edition limited to 100 copies only was
released in 1999, by the author (Ross Strachan).
This scarce work contains *"How Jack the Ripper
Was Caught: The Full Inside Story"*.

WOODHALL
Edwin Thomas

Jack the Ripper: or When London Walked in Terror.

Mellifont Press, Chancery Lane, London.

First published on 20th April 1937 as part of their Celebrated Crime Series (No. 14). A pulp paperback in large format (8.5"x5.5"). Copies are now very scarce and collectors may struggle to find a copy. It was reprinted by Mellifont on 10th November 1938 in a slightly smaller format. It was again reprinted by Mellifont, who had since moved to Furnival Street, on 20th March 1949 as part of their Tower Series (No. 14). Again, it was in a smaller size (7"x4.75").
In 1997 P&D Riley Publishers of Runcorn produced a facsimile edition of the original 1937 edition in a limited edition run, comprising of 500 copies. The only difference, and a significant one, was that the 1997 issue had a new front cover and not the original showing the Ripper poised to attack a woman in the street.
Woodhall asks whether Jack the Ripper was actually Jill the Ripper, namely Olga Tchkersoff.
A rather fictitious look at the events in Whitechapel.

STEWART William

Jack the Ripper: A New Theory.

Quality Press, London, 1939.
William Saunders, Toronto, Canada, 1939.

A hardback book which looks at the murders in twenty six chapters and also boasts fourteen illustrations including portraits of the victims painted by the author from contemporary sketches. Stewart also made models of some of the murder sites from original plans and sketches.
This is without doubt the most sought after Ripper book which is now very scarce. Copies rarely turn up for sale and, when they do, can command a high asking price due to the fact that the book is thought to have had a small print run.

Stewart's theory was that the Whitechapel Murderer was not a man, but a woman – possibly a crazed midwife. Sir Arthur Conan Doyle also favoured this theory.

BARNARD Allan
(Editor)

The Harlot Killer: Jack the Ripper in Fact and Fiction.

First published Dodd and Mead, New York, USA 1953 H/B.
Reprinted Dell Books, New York, USA, 1953 P/B
(No. 797) under the title 'The World's Most Diabolical Murderer: The Harlot Killer'.

Both the hardback and paperback copies of this work are fairly hard to obtain especially in the UK as it was never published outside America. The P/B has a rather attractive cover showing the Ripper attacking his "attractive, well dressed victim".

Of the thirteen short stories contained in the anthology four are factual accounts:

i) Murder Unlimited - Alan Hynd

ii) The Jack the Ripper Murders -Edited Richard Barker

iii) Frenchy: Ameer Ben Ali by Edwin M. Borchard

iv) Jack the Ripper - Edmund Pearson.

McCORMICK
Donald

The Identity of Jack the Ripper

Jarrolds, London, 1959 H/B.
Great Pan Books, London, 1962 P/B
(No. 9542)

Revised Editions
John Long, London, 1970, H/B
Arrow Books, London, 1970 P/B (No. 374)
Second Impression - April 1971.

Extra Edition
Boots Booklovers Library Edition
A Book Club edition produced around 1960 in H/B with no dustjacket.

Most of the above titles are easily located although the John Long 1970 H/B is fairly scarce these days. The Arrow paperbacks have the same cover as the John Long dustjacket. McCormick names Dr. Alexander Pedachenko as Jack the Ripper, however, he places too much emphasis on the Doctor Dutton diaries which he claims to have once seen. Most researchers are wary of these diaries which have never been proved to exist.

CULLEN Tom

Autumn of Terror: Jack the Ripper - His Crimes and Times.
Bodley Head Ltd., London, 1965.

A hardback also reprinted in 1965 as well as a third impression produced towards the end of the year. In 1966 a paperback was released by Fontana Books, London, (No. 1357) Cullen's book was also printed in America although it had a new title - *When London Walked in Terror.*
No less than five impressions were released in 1965 by publisher Houghton Mifflin and Company of Boston. In the States the book was described as "a masterful study of Jack the Ripper and a Victorian England powerless before him". A paperback followed in February 1968, under the same title, published by Avon Books, New York, (No. V2177). It ran to three separate printings with the third printing having a slightly different cover. Back in the UK another paperback edition was published in 1973 by Fontana Books, London, under the title '*The Crimes and Times of Jack the Ripper*" (No. 3403). The cover showed actor Chris Fenwick as John Richardson in the first episode of the BBC tv series Jack the Ripper.
All of the different editions of Cullen's work are easily obtainable. Rather surprisingly, Cullen never once revised his original 1965 offering which names Montague Druitt as the Ripper. Tom Cullen went on to state "I stopped being interested in the identity of Jack the Ripper when it became a cottage industry".

ODELL Robin   *Jack the Ripper in Fact and Fiction.*
                                      Harrap and Co., London, 1965 H/B.
                                      Mayflower Dell, London, 1966 P/B
                                      (No.4195)

                      **Both editions are obtainable today although the hardback
                      will be slightly more difficult to trace.   The paperback
                      issued in September 1966 was indeed revised and contained
                      a new chapter entitled 'Gentleman Jack'.**
                      **A major work which came to the conclusion that Jack was
                      an unknown shochet or Jewish slaughterman residing in
                      the area.**

FARSON Daniel   *Jack the Ripper.*
                                      Michael Joseph Ltd., London, 1972,
                                      H/B.

                      **Reprinted again in 1972 and 1973 in hardback.   A
                      hardback version was also issued around 1973 by the
                      History Book Club, London.   A revised paperback was
                      published in 1973 by Sphere Books Ltd., London, which
                      agreed with the earlier work by Cullen that Montague
                      Druitt was responsible for the Ripper killings. However,
                      Farson's was the first book to include mortuary
                      photographs of the victims.**

HARRISON
Michael   *Clarence: The Life of H.R.H. The Duke of
                      Clarence and Avondale 1864 - 1892.*
                                      W.H. Allen, London, 1972, H/B.

                      Published under the title:
                      Clarence - Was he Jack the Ripper?
                      Drake Publishing Inc., New York, USA, 1974, H/B.
                      **Harrison points the finger at J.K. Stephen in this
                      biography.   The UK edition is the more difficult of the
                      two to obtain.   There is a distinct possibility that the
                      American edition may have been remaindered at one
                      time.**

KELLY Alexander   *Jack the Ripper: A Bibliography and*
Review of the Literature.
Association of Assistant Librarians,
South East Dept., London, 1973, P/B
(Card Covers).
Revised: 1984 H/B and 1995 P/B.

**A work no serious collector of Jack the Ripper should be
without. All editions open with "An introduction To The
Murders and Theories" by Colin Wilson, and list many
Ripper books, both factual and fictional, published since
the murders occurred. The revised 1995 edition is the
most informative although it does not include many Ripper
items published before 1995 and lists some titles which are
scarcely related to Jack the Ripper. However it does
include a chapter by Kelly and David Sharp which looks
at the life of the Ripper in music, films and television.
Of all three editions the 1984 hardback is the most difficult
to locate.**

WHITTINGTON-
EGAN   *The Identity of Jack the Ripper.*
Richard   Reprinted from the Contemporary
Review 1973
Booklet (Red Covers with Black
Lettering).
Limited to only 100 numbered copies.

**A scarce and collectable nineteen page booklet where the
author decides that the two most likely candidates would
seem to be Pedachenko and Druitt, although there is not
substantial evidence to warrant a conviction.**

RAPER Michell

Who Was Jack the Ripper?
The Tabaret Press, London, 1974,
Booklet.
Limited to 100 numbered copies.

A resume of the Whitechapel Murders of 1888 and an investigation of a recent suspect. The script of this publication was broadcast on BBC Radio Four on 1st June 1972.

WHITTINGTON-
EGAN
Richard

A Casebook on Jack the Ripper.
Wildy and Sons, London, 1975 H/B.

A hardback beautifully produced in red boards with gold lettering which is now fairly scarce and a collectable Ripper title. Only around 700 copies are thought to have been published. The author reviews all of the literature published prior to 1975.

JONES Elwyn and
LLOYD John

The Ripper File.
Arthur Barker Ltd., London, 1975 H/B.
Futura Publications Ltd., London, 1975,
P/B.

Both books were published simultaneously and are hard to locate. Most copies of the hardback which turn up seem to be ex-library copies. Not illustrated. A documentary investigation by the fictional Detectives Charles Barlow and John Watt.

RUMBELOW
Donald

The Complete Jack the Ripper
W.H. Allen, London, 1975, H/B.
Star Books, London, 1976, P/B.

Reprinted and slightly revised Star Books, London, 1981 and 1984 paperbacks. Published in America in 1975 in a large sized hardback by the New York Graphical Society of Boston, Massachusetts and also in a smaller size as a Book Club Edition. In September 1976 the first American paperback was published by Signet Books, New York, (No. J7148) and, unlike the British paperbacks, this edition carried the introduction by Colin Wilson. In September 1987 W.H. Allen, London, published a new and completely revised hardback edition which proved so popular that it was republished again in December of the same year. A Book Club edition was also released in hardback in 1987 by Guild Publishing using the same dustjacket as the W.H. Allen edition. The revised paperback edition was published by Penguin Books, London, in 1988 and has been reprinted many times since. It also carried an addendum which looked at Martin Fido's suspect Aaron Kosminski. In America the revised book was retitled *'Jack the Ripper The Complete Casebook'* and published in hardback by Contemporary Books Inc., Chicago, in 1988. A paperback edition was issued by Berkley Books of New York in July 1990.Rumbelow is a true Ripper expert and his book was very well received. He offers no name to the identity of Jack the Ripper. A well written and researched work and well worth tracking down.

KNIGHT Stephen   *Jack the Ripper: The Final Solution.*
                                George Harrup and Co., London, 1976
                                reprinted 1979.

Revised and reprinted again in 1984 by Treasure Press, London, in a hardback with laminated boards. No dust jacket was issued with this edition.   First issued in paperback form by Granada/Grafton Books,   London in 1977 and reprinted countless times since.
In America the book was first issued by David McKay and Co., New York in 1976 with a different dustjacket to the UK edition and an American paperback was released in 1986 by Chicago Academy Publishing of Chicago.
Of all the Ripper books this is probably the best known. Knight implicates the Freemasons as being involved in the Ripper murders as well as exposing a Royal connection. Fanciful stuff, nevertheless a popular book.

SPIERING Frank   *Prince Jack: The True Story of Jack the Ripper.*
                                Doubleday & Co., Inc., New York,
                                USA,1978 H/B.
                                Jove Books, New York, USA, April
                                1980
                                Paperback, (No. B5496).

A book never published outside of America which comes to the conclusion that the Duke of Clarence, Queen Victoria's grandson, was responsible for the killings.

DOUGLAS Arthur   *Will the Real Jack the Ripper.*
                                    Countryside Publications Ltd., Chorley,
                                    Lancs, 1979.

**Published in both hardback and paperback this short but
informative book is worth tracking down. The author
does not put a suspect forward but provides a good account
of the murders. The hardback was released with
laminated boards and was never issued with a dustjacket.**

**The paperback used the exact same cover. The book was
also released in Audio Cassette form in 1979 in 2 x 45
minute sides.**

JINKO Katsuo   *Terror in London - on Jack the Ripper and His Time*
                                    Japan, Post 1981, H/B.

**An eminent Japanese criminologist discusses the case in
this very hard to locate title. A dustjacket was issued with
this edition.**

FIDO Martin   *The Crimes Detection and Death of
Jack the Ripper.*
                                    Weidenfeld and Nicolson, London,
                                    1987, H/B.

**In 1989 the same company released a paperback version
which was revised and updated. It was also reprinted in
1993 by Orion Books Ltd., London, with a different cover.
The American edition was published in hardback in 1993
by Barnes and Noble Books, New York with a different
dustjacket to it's UK counterpart. It contained a brand
new preface written in 1993 where Fido looked at some of
the Ripper works published since his book was revised in
1989.**
**Fido puts forward Nathan Kaminsky a.k.a. David Cohen
as a suspect.**

MARX Roland   *Jack L'Eventreur et Les Fantasmes Victoriens.*
         Editions Complexe, Brussels, Belgium,
         1987, (No. 204), P/B.

A French work although published in Belgium in which a French Professor discusses the Ripper and his crimes. Hard to locate, especially in the UK and America.

HARRIS Melvin   *Jack the Ripper:The Bloody Truth.*
         Columbus Books, London, 1987, H/B.

A work never reprinted or released in paperback where Harris points the finger at Dr. Roslyn D'Onston Stephenson as being Jack the Ripper. The book itself is rather unique as it is the only book connected with the case to boast a competition on the dustjacket, relating to his theory. Apparently it was not won.

HOWELLS Martin   *The Ripper Legacy: The Life and Death of Jack*
SKINNER Keith &   *The Ripper.*
         Sidgwick & Jackson Ltd., London,
         1987, H/B.
         Reprinted October 1987.

First published in paperback form by Sphere Books, London in 1988 also reprinted that year. It was again reprinted in 1992 by Warner Books, London, using the same cover. An American paperback was released in 1988 by Viking/Penguin, New York.
Another interesting edition which exists is a large print edition in hardback, published by Chivers Press, Bath, for the Library Association which used a completely different dustjacket to the original.
The authors once again put forward Montague Druitt as the Ripper in a book which published previously unseen photographs of Druitt and his family (H/B only).

SHARKEY	*Jack the Ripper: 100 Years of Investigation.*
Terrence	Wardlock Ltd., London, 1987, H/B.
	Dorset Press, New York, USA, 1992, H/B.
	(US edition has a different dustjacket).

A rather poor book which offers no new information regarding the case. It was probably only produced to cash in on the forthcoming centenary of the murders. The American edition has a really distinctive Ripper cover.

UNDERWOOD	
Peter	*Jack the Ripper: 100 Years of Mystery.*
	Blandford Press, London, 1987, H/B.
	Javelin Books, London, 1988, P/B.

The author offers no new information but gives a good account of the murders, where he favours Joseph Barnett as the culprit. The book also gives us three other views on the killings by James Tully, Peter Rowe and Sean Day. An enjoyable read. The hardback version can be tricky to locate.

WILSON Colin &	*Jack the Ripper: Summing Up and Verdict.*
ODELL Robin	Bantam Press, London, 1987, H/B.
	Corgi Books, London, 1988, P/B.
	Reprinted 1988, 1990, 1991, 1992.

An excellent reworking of the case with no favoured suspect and no new theories put forward, although a few errors are included.

CROWLEY Aleister   *Jack the Ripper.*

Privately printed booklet.
Cambridge, August 1988.
Limited to 100 copies only.

The infamous Crowley gives his thoughts on Jack the Ripper in this very collectable booklet. It was first published as an article in 'Sothis' (Vol. 1 No. 4 1974)

MORRISON
John   *Jimmy Kelly's Year of Ripper Murders 1888.*

Privately printed booklet, London, 1988.

A rather tame offering which suggests James Kelly as being the Whitechapel Murderer.

BEGG Paul   *Jack the Ripper: The Uncensored Facts.*

Robson Books, London, 1988, H/B.
Robson Books, London, 1989, P/B.
Reprinted 1989, 1990, 1991, 1992, 1993, 1994, 1995 and 1996.

A very competent account of the Ripper murders. Also the only title to be published in the centenary year. Favours Kosminski.

HARRIS Melvin   *The Ripper File.*

W.H. Allen, London, 1989, H/B.

Mostly contains contemporary newspaper articles relating to the case.

THOMAS Lars   *Mysteriet om Jack the Ripper.*
                                Gyldendal, Copenhagen, Denmark,
                                1990, P/B.

A short but informative account aimed at the younger
audience by Denmark's leading Ripper expert.

COLBY-NEWTON   *Jack the Ripper: Opposing Viewpoints.*
Katie   Greenhaven Press, San Diego,
                                California, USA, 1990, H/B.
                                No dustjacket.

Published as part of a 'Great Mysteries' series, this
competent work is aimed at the younger audience.

HARRISON Paul   *Jack the Ripper: The Mystery Solved.*
                                Robert Hale Ltd., London, 1991, H/B.
                                Robert Hale Ltd., London, 1993, P/B.

Joseph Barnett is identified as the culprit in this work
which can be fairly difficult to locate.

FULLER   *Sickert and The Ripper Crimes.*
Jean Overton   Mandrake Press, Oxford, 1990, H/B.

The artist Walter Sickert is claimed to be solely responsible
for the killings.

FAIRCLOUGH   *The Ripper and The Royals.*
Melvyn   Duckworth & Co., London, 1991 H/B
                                Also released in hardback as a second
                                impression in 1992.
                                Duckworth & Co., London, 1992 P/B
                                edition - fully corrected and augmented.

A reworking of the Stephen Knight theory, however
Lord Randolph Churchill is blamed for the killings.

BEGG Paul, FIDO Martin & SKINNER Keith	*The Jack the Ripper A-Z.* Headline, London, 1991, H/B Revised - Headline, London, 1992, P/B. Revised - Headline, London, 1994, P/B. Revised - Headline, London, 1996, P/B.

A must for every enthusiasts bookshelves. Lists all the main characters and events relating to the murders in alphabetical order.

ABRAHAMSEN Dr. David	*Murder and Madness: The Secret Life of Jack the Ripper.* Robson Books, London, 1992, H/B. Donald Fine, New York, USA, 1992, H/B. Avon Books, New York, USA, 1993, P/B. Robson Books, London, 1994, P/B.

The author claimed to base the book on heretofore unrevealed information from Scotland Yard, and concluded that J.K. Stephen and Prince Eddy were jointly responsible for the murders.

BOURGOIN Stephane	*Jack L'Eventreur.* Fleuve Noir, Paris, France, 1992, P/B.

Editions De Cremille, Geneva, 1997, H/B, no dustjacket. Issued in black leather and gold boards. This edition was actually a Book Club issue. Leading French expert surveys the case.

HARRISON Shirley	*The Diary of Jack the Ripper. The Discovery, The Investigation, The Authentification.*
	Smith Gryphon Ltd., London, 1993, H/B.
	No dustjacket issued.
	Reprinted 1993, 1994, 1995, 1996 and 1997.
	Book Club Associates, London, 1993, H/B.
	No dustjacket issued.
	Index Book Club, London, 1994, H/B.
	Issued with dustjacket.
	Smith Gryphon Ltd., London, 1994, P/B.
	Reprinted 1996.
	New introduction by Colin Wilson.
	Blake Publishing, London, 1998, P/B.
	Updated and revised edition.
	American Editions - Hyperion, New York, 1993, H/B, issued with dustjacket.
	Pocket Books, New York, 1995, P/B.

Based on a diary discovered which was supposedly written by Liverpool cotton merchant James Maybrick who claimed to be Jack the Ripper. The diary has fuelled much debate and today it is unclear whether it is genuine or an elaborate hoax!

WOLF A.P.	*Jack the Myth: A New Look at The Ripper.*
	Robert Hale Ltd., London, 1993, H/B.
	Also Large Print Edition by Cedric Chivers, Bath, 1994, H/B. Same dustjacket as original.

The mysterious A.P. Wolf blames Thomas Cutbush for the killings in this now hard to find book.

ACHAD OSHER 583   *Did Aleister Crowley Know the Identity of*
FRATER   *Jack the Ripper?*

Pangenetor Lodge Publications,
California, USA,1994, Pamphlet/
Booklet.
Originally privately published by
Cornelius (USA) in December 1993.

A scarce booklet which looks at the connection between Crowley and Ripper killings.

WILDING John   *Jack the Ripper Revealed.*

Constable/Volcano Books, London,
1993, H/B.
Constable/Volcano Books, London,
1993, P/B.

Montague Druitt and J.K. Stephen are put forward as the killers in this work which might interest crossword puzzle buffs!

CORY Patricia   *An Eye To The Future.*

Privately printed by D&P Cory,
Norwich, 1993 in dossier form.
First edition limited to 100 copies.
Second edition - 500 copies at the
most.

The author believes that the murders were part of a masonic conspiracy which is backed up by a document called "The Lost Affidavit of James Avery" in which Avery swears that the crimes were committed by the Freemasons.

SUGDEN Philip   *The Complete History of Jack the Ripper.*
Robinson Publishing, London, 1994,
H/B.
A Book Club Edition by Book Club
Associates was also released with same
dustjacket.
Robinson Publishing, London, 1995,
P/B.
Carroll & Graf, New York, 1994, H/B.
Revised issue with identical dustjacket
to UK edition.
Carroll & Graf, New York, 1995, P/B,
revised edition.

A must for every Ripper enthusiast. A brilliantly written and researched work which must rate amongst the best books written on the subject. Possibly only let down by favouring George Chapman as the most likely suspect.

HARRIS Melvin   *The True Face of Jack the Ripper.*
Michael O'Mara. London, 1994, H/B.
Michael O'Mara, London, 1995, P/B.

Harris's third work devoted to the case where he once again concentrates on his suspect Dr. Roslyn D'Onston Stephenson.

DE LOCKSLEY   *The Enigma of Jack the Ripper.*
Dr. John   Privately published, London, 1995
Folder/Dossier form. Red covers with
black comb binding.

The author looks at the crimes and suspects in this hard to find work.

DE LOCKSLEY   *Jack the Ripper Unveiled.*
Dr. John   Privately published, London, 1995.
                                       Folder/Dossier form.   Red covers with
                                       red comb binding.

The author again looks at the case and reveals his
preferred suspect, a Doctor Hewlett.

WOLFF Camille   *Who Was Jack the Ripper? A Collection of Present-*
                                Day Theories and Observations.
                                       Grey House Books, London, 1995,
                                       H/B
                                       Limited to 100 copies only in an edition
                                       signed by all fifty three contributors.
                                       Grey House Books, London, 1995,
                                       H/B.
                                       Reprint edition unsigned by the fifty
                                       three contributors.   Limited to 1000
                                       copies.

Specialist crime bookseller Camille Wolff produced and
edited this book which features fifty three Ripper experts
giving their views on the murders.   The contributors
included Stewart Evans, Paul Begg, Donald Rumbelow and
Martin Fido. Loretta Lay of Grey House Books must also
take credit for producing this book which no collector
should be without.

EVANS Stewart &   *The Lodger: The Arrest and Escape of*
GAINEY Paul   *Jack the Ripper.*
                                       Century Ltd., London, 1995, H/B.
                                       An edition by Book Club Associates
                                       also released, same dustjacket.
                                       Retitled - *Jack the Ripper: First*
                                       American Serial Killer.
                                       Arrow Books, London, 1996, P/B, fully
                                       revised.Kodansha, New York, USA,
                                       1996, H/B. Different dustjacket to UK
                                       edition. Kodansha, New York, USA,
                                       1998, P/B.

The authors put forward an American quack doctor named Francis Tumblety as the culprit. Their research was based on a letter written by ex Chief Inspector John Littlechild in 1913 to George Sims which named Tumblety. Very refreshing to see a very viable new suspect put forward. The American hardback edition by Kodansha is a must for serious Ripper collectors.

PALEY Bruce — *Jack the Ripper: The Simple Truth.*
> Headline Publishing, London, 1995, Oversized (trade) paperback.
> Headline Publishing, London, 1996, P/B.

Paley names Joseph Barnett as the killer in this well researched work. Of the two editions the trade paperback edition is the most difficult to locate.

BEADLE William — *Jack the Ripper: Anatomy of A Myth.*
> Wat Tyler Books, Dagenham, Essex, 1995, H/B.

The first book to name William Henry Bury as the Ripper. Bury was hanged in Scotland for the murder of his wife.

PALMER Scott — *Jack the Ripper: A Reference Guide.*
> Scarecrow Press Inc., Maryland, USA, and Folkestone, England, 1995, H/B, not issued with a dustjacket.

Palmer looks at all the main characters involved with the case.

GREGORY Roy   *Jack The Ripper And Victorian London.*
                              Elm Publications, Cambridgeshire, UK,
                              August 1995, Wolf Pack,
                              No. W60 KS2.

**An educational pack which discusses the Ripper murders
and the era in which they were committed. Through a
series of mainly single sided pages containing diagrams,
illustrations and writings, the reader can obtain most of
the basic facts surrounding the case.**
**A rather obscure and little known work contained in a
plastic folder.**
The series editor was Pauline Hornsby.

FISHER Peter   *An Illustrated Guide to Jack the Ripper.*
                              P&D Riley, Runcorn, Cheshire, 1996,
                              H/B, not issued with a dustjacket:
                              laminated boards.
                              P&D Riley, Runcorn, Cheshire, 1996,
                              P/B, (same cover as hardback version).

**A heavily illustrated account of the murders.   Offers
nothing new regarding the case.**

DE LOCKSLEY   *A Ramble With Jack the Ripper.*
Dr. John   Privately published, London, 1996,
                              Folder/Dossier form.

**The authors' third 'book' on the case where he concludes
George Chapman as the most likely suspect.**

STRACHAN Ross   *Jack the Ripper: A Collectors Guide To The Many*
                        Books Published.
                                        Privately Published, Galston, Scotland,
                                        November 1996, Folder/Dossier Form.
                                        Limited to 100 Copies.
                                        Revised and updated edition May 1997.
                                        Limited to 100 copies.

                        **Both factual and fictional works are included in a book
                        which was aimed at collectors. Availability and value were
                        also discussed.**

SUGDEN Philip   *The Life and Times of Jack the Ripper.*
                                        Sienna/Parragon, Bristol, 1996, H/B.

                        **A miniature book measuring 4.5"x3.5" which was issued,
                        with a dustjacket, at a bargain price. A short look at the
                        murders.**

WALLACE Richard   *Jack the Ripper: Lighthearted Friend.*
                                        Gemini Press, Melrose, USA, 1996,
                                        P/B.
                                        Gazelle Publishing, London, 1997, P/B.

                        **Lewis Carroll, creator of Alice in Wonderland; real name
                        Charles Lutwidge Dodgson, is named as a possible suspect.**

TURNBULL Peter   *The Killer Who Never Was.*
                                        Clark, Lawrence Publishers, Hull, 1996,
                                        H/B. No dustjacket - black boards.

                        **A hard to find title, due to it's small print run, in which
                        Turnbull takes an overall look at the Whitechapel Murders.**

FELDMAN Paul   *Jack the Ripper: The Final Chapter.*
                                  Virgin Publishing, London, 1997, H/B.
                                  Virgin Publishing, London, 1998, P/B.

Feldman sets out to prove that the Jack the Ripper diary is genuine and was indeed penned by the killer - James Maybrick.

O'DONNELL Kevin   *The Jack the Ripper Whitechapel Murders.*
                                  Ten Bells Publishing, Essex, 1997, H/B.

Based on the research of Andy and Sue Parlour this recommended work gives an overview of the case with 'new' information on Sir William Gull and others. Two different dustjackets exist. The original jacket was altered to give more prominence to the hard work put in by the Parlours.

TULLY James   *The Secret of Prisoner 1167: Was This Man*
                      Jack the Ripper?
                                  Robinson Publishing, London, 1997,
                                  H/B.
                                  Robinson Publishing, London, 1998,
                                  P/B.
                      Released in America as -
                      Prisoner 1167: The Madman Who Was Jack the
                      Ripper.
                                  Carroll and Graf, New York, 1997,
                                  H/B.
                                  Carroll and Graf, New York, 1998,
                                  P/B.

The author puts forward James Kelly, who escaped from Broadmoor, as being responsible for the murders.

SPEHNER Norbert   *Les Fils De Jack L'Eventreur.*
                                    Nuit Blanche Editeur, Quebec, Canada,
                                    1996, P/B.

                   **Translated as 'The Sons of Jack the Ripper': this is a
                   bibliography written entirely in French which looks at some
                   of the novels written featuring serial killers including Jack
                   the Ripper.**

TROW M.J.   *The Many Faces of Jack the Ripper.*
                                    Summersdale Publishers, West Sussex,
                                    1997, H/B.
                                    Summersdale Publishers, West Sussex,
                                    1998, P/B.

                   **A wonderfully illustrated book which takes a look at the
                   Ripper murders and the area in which they were
                   committed.   Photography by Tim Craddock.**

DEW Walter   *The Hunt for Jack the Ripper.*
                                    Privately published by Dave Froggatt,
                                    Birmingham, UK, 1998, Booklet.

                   **Dew's book *"I caught Crippen"* published in 1938 by
                   Blackie, London, had one third of it devoted to the Ripper
                   case.   Froggatt has taken the relevant pages and produced
                   this facsimile edition.   The original 1938 work is hard to
                   find these days, so this edition is most welcome.**

BOURGOIN
Stephane   *Le Livre Rouge De Jack L'Eventreur.*
                                    Bernard Grasset, Paris, France,
                                    1998, P/B.

                   **French Ripper expert Bourgoin's second book on the case.
                   Translated as *"The Red Book of Jack the Ripper"* it is a
                   mixture of both fact and fiction and also boasts an
                   impressive bibliography.   The factual section is entitled
                   *"L'enigme de Jack L'Eventreur".***

| HINTON Bob | *From Hell: The Jack the Ripper Mystery.* |
| | Old Bakehouse Publications, Gwent, Wales, June 1998, P/B. |

The author believes the Ripper to be George Hutchinson, a well known name in the case.

| RYDER Stephen (Editor) | *The First Fifty Years of Jack the Ripper: Volume One.* |
| | Ripperological Preservation Society, Paramus, New Jersey, USA, 1998, Pamphlet. |

Includes relevant Ripper sections reprinted from the following sources:
i)   **Sir Melville Macnaghten, Days of My Years, 1914.**
ii) **H.L. Adam, The Police Encyclopaedia, 1920.**
iii) **H.L. Adam, The Trial of George Chapman, 1930.**
iv) **George Sims, Mysteries of Modern London, 1906.**
v) **George Sims, My Life - Sixty Years, 1917**
vi) **L. Forbes Winslow, Recollections of Forty Years, 1910**

| RYDER Stephen (Editor) | *The First Fifty Years of Jack the Ripper: Volume Two.* |
| | Ripperological Preservation Society, Paramus, New Jersey, USA, 1998, Pamphlet. |

Includes relevant Ripper sections reprinted from the following sources:
i)   **Montagu Williams - Later Leaves, 1891.**
ii) **Arthur Griffiths - Mysteries of Police and Crime, 1898.**
iii) **Sir Robert Anderson - The Lighter Side of my Official Life, 1910.**
iv) **H.L. Adam - Police Work from Within, 1914.**
v) **J. Rowland Brookes - Murder in Fact & Fiction, 1925.**
vi) **F.P. Wensley - Detective Days, 1933.**
vii) **E. Pearson - More Studies in Murder, 1936.**

SMITHKEY III
John

Jack the Ripper: The Inquest of The Final
Victim Mary Kelly.

> Key Publications, Ohio, USA, 1998,
> H/B.
> Key Publications, Ohio, USA, 1998,
> P/B, same cover as hardback.

The book contains the actual facsimile of both the witness testimonies of the coroner's inquest and witness statements taken on the morning of Kelly's murder. Includes some of Stewart Evans' 1967 collection of photographs showing the murder sites.

BALL Pamela

Jack the Ripper: A Psychic Investigation -
The Compelling Paranormal Search For
The Killers True Identity.

> Arcturus Publishing, Leicester, 1998,
> H/B.

The author uses both astrology and channelling to shed some light on the Ripper mystery. These methods seem a little unusual or even far-fetched for many cynics, including myself I'm afraid.

PLIMMER John F.

In The Footsteps of the Whitechapel Murders:
An Examination of the Jack the Ripper Murders Using
Modern Police Techniques.

> Book Guild Ltd., Sussex, 1998, H/B.
> Book Guild Ltd., Sussex, 1998, P/B.

A book which attempts to solve the crimes using modern police methods and which also appears to mix fiction with fact. Due to a small print run the hardback sold out very quickly and is now hard to locate.

| PATTERSON | *Paradox: Upon Jack the Ripper Poetry and Francis* |
| Richard | *Joseph Thompson.* |

Privately published, Melbourne, Victoria, Australia, 1998, Booklet/ Dossier Form.
Originally published in Australia as *Requiem.*

Patterson introduces English poet Francis Thompson as a suspect in the Whitechapel Murders.

WRIGHT Stephen   *Jack the Ripper - An American View.*

Mystery Notebook Editions, New York, USA, 1999, P/B.
First Edition limited to 150 copies.

George Hutchinson is put forward as being responsible for the Ripper killings. The author also rules out Tumblety, Maybrick and George Chapman as possible culprits.

GRAHAM Anne E.   *The Last Victim: The Extraordinary Life of*
EMMAS Carol   *Florence Maybrick, the wife of Jack the Ripper.*

Headline Publishing, London, UK, 1999.

This book is a biography of Florence Maybrick, wife of James Maybrick who many believe was Jack the Ripper, due to the Ripper Diary discovered in 1992, which was supposedly written by James Maybrick.   Chapter four deals with the Ripper case.

JAKUBOWSKI
Maxim
BRAUND Nathan
(Editors)

The Mammoth Book of Jack the Ripper.
Robinson Publishing, London, UK,
1999, P/B

Sixteen authorities on the mystery of Jack the Ripper give their views in this anthology which also takes an overall look at the case. Contributors include William Beadle, Paul Harrison, Sue and Andy Parlour and Nick Warren.

ROGERS Brian
(Editor).

Reflections On The Ripper: Four Accounts Of The Whitechapel Murders.
Privately published booklet, by Brian Rogers, Brighton,1999.

Mr. Rogers has written a short introduction to this work which contains the relevant Jack the Ripper sections taken from the following four books:
i). Tom Divall – *Scoundrels And Scallywags.*
ii). Ben Leeson – *Lost London.*
iii). Parrish and Crossland – *The Fifty Most Amazing Crimes Of The Last 100 Years.*
(F.A. Beaumont – *The Fiend Of East London – Jack the Ripper).*
iv). W.B. Hill – *A New Earth And A New Heaven.*

COLVILLE Gary &
LUCANIO Patrick

Jack The Ripper: His Life And Crimes In Popular Entertainment.
McFarland & Co.,Carolina, USA,
1999.

This book is an extensive overview of the many fictional treatments of the case found in all types of media, from novels to television and radio. The many films are also discussed. Recommended for factual students of the case also.

A number of the well known factual studies of the Whitechapel Murders have been translated and published abroad.

The following works are prime examples.

CULLEN Tom   *Jack L'Eventreur*
                              Deneol, Paris, France, 1965.

CULLEN Tom   *I Angstens Skygge: Da Jack the Ripper Spredte*
                              Raedsel Over Dronning Victoria's London.
                              Schultz-Kobenhaven, Copenhagen,
                              Denmark, 1966.

ODELL Robin   *Jack the Ripper.*
                              Kramers Pockets Van Formaat,
                              Netherlands, 1966, P/B. (No. 29).

CULLEN Tom   *Jack the Ripper: Der Morder Von London.*
                              Lagen Muller, Munich, Germany, 1967.
                              Ullstein Buch, Frankfurt, Germany,
                              1970, P/B, (No. 2759).   Reprinted 1988
                              different cover (No. 980) - again re
                              printed in 1990.

CULLEN Tom   *Jack the Ripper Slaat Toe.*
                              Walter Beckers, Antwerp, Belgium,
                              1972.

HARRIS Melvin   *Jack the Ripper: Die Blutige Wahreit 100 Jahre Danach.*
                              Hannibal Publishers, Germany, 1988.

HARRISON Shirley   *Het Dagboek Van Jack the Ripper.*
                              Uitgeveriy Łuitingh, Amsterdam,
                              Netherlands, 1993, P/B.

WILDING John   *Jack the Ripper: Des Ratsels Losung.*
                                    Schneekluth, Munich, Germany, 1994.

HARRISON Shirley   *Das Tagebuch Von Jack the Ripper.*
                                    Bastei Lubbe, Munich, Germany, 1994,
                                    reprinted 1995, 1996, 1997.
                                    Bastei Lubbe, Munich, Germany, 1998,
                                    P/B, (No. 13 980).

HARRISON Shirley   *Kirisaki Jakku No Nikki*
                                    Tokoyo, Japan, 1994.

The 'diary' translated by Tsumuyuki Serizowa and Akiko Ono.

HARRISON Shirley   *Le Journal De Jack L'Eventreur.*
                                    Editions Jean Claude Lettes, Paris,
                                    France, 1993.
                                    Le Livre De Poche, Paris, France,
                                    1995.

PALEY Bruce   *Jack the Ripper: The Simple Truth.*
                                    Japan, 1997.

A hardback with dustjacket printed and published in Japan.   Translated into Japanese by the English Agency (Japan) Ltd.

THE

Whitechapel ❧

❧ Atrocities.

ARREST

OF A

Newspaper Reporter.

PRICE ONE PENNY.

WOODFORD FAWCETT & Co.
DORSET WORKS, SALISBURY SQUARE, LONDON, E.C.

ENTERED AT STATIONERS' HALL.   COPYRIGHT.

The
Whitechapel Atrocities.
An early work published in
1888.

**Jack The Ripper:
Or When London Walked In
Terror
Edwin T. Woodhall.**
This illustration shows the third
edition issued in 1949.

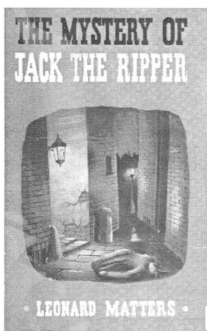

The Mystery of
Jack the Ripper
by
Leonard Matters.
An early work published in
1948 W.H. Allen dustjacket.

Jack the Ripper:
A New Theory
by
William Stewart.
1939 Quality Press dustjacket.

Jack L'Eventreur
by Roland Marx.
Editions Complexe, 1987.

Mysteriet Om
Jack the Ripper
by Lars Thomas 1990.

Jack L'Eventreur
by Stephane Bourgoin.
Fleuve Noir, 1992 paperback.

Jack the Myth
by A.P. Wolf
1993.

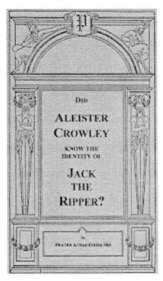

Did Aleister Crowley Know
The Identity of Jack The
Ripper? by Frater Achad
Oscher 583 1994.

From Hell
by
Bob Hinton.

Jack the Ripper
by Robin Odell
Dutch 1966 paperback edition.

Jack the Ripper:
Der Morder Von London
by Tom Cullen.
Ullstein Buch, Germany, 1970
paperback.

CHAPTER THREE.

OTHER RELEVANT TITLES

The amount of material written about the Whitechapel Murders is huge, and as well as factual studies devoted to the case there are many other works worth collecting as they are invaluable to the case. True crime books and police biographies are just two areas where we find many references to the Ripper case.

WILLIAMS Montagu	*Later Leaves.*	MacMillan, London, UK, 1891.
MacDONALD Arthur	*Criminology.*	Funk and Wagnalls, USA, 1893.
GRIFFITHS Arthur G.F.	*Mysteries of Police and Crime.*	Cassell, London, UK, 1898.
SIMS George	*Mysteries of Modern London.*	Pearson, London, UK, 1906.
ANDERSON Sir Robert	*Criminals and Crime: Some Facts and Suggestions.*	Nisbet, London, UK, 1907.
ANDERSON Sir Robert	*The Lighter Side of My Official Life.*	Hodder & Stoughton, London, UK, 1910. Also Hodder & Stoughton, New York, USA, 1911.

SMITH Sir Henry	*From Constable to Commissioner: The Story of Sixty Years, Most of Them Misspent.*	
		Chatto & Windass, London, UK, 1910.

WINSLOW L. Forbes	*Recollections of Forty Years.*	
		John Ouseley Ltd., London, UK, 1910.

MacNAGHTEN Sir Melville	*Days of My Years.*	
		Edward Arnold, London, UK, 1914.
		Also Longmans, USA, 1914.

SIMS George	*My Life: Sixty Years.*	
	Recollections of Bohemian London.	
		Eveleigh Nash Company, London, UK, 1917.

LE QUEUX William	*Things I Know About Kings, Celebrities and Crooks.*	
		Eveleigh Nash & Grayson Ltd, London, UK, 1923
		also Frederick A. Stokes Co., New York, USA,
		(not dated) 1923.

BROOKS John A.R.	*Murder In Fact And Fiction.*	
		Hurst and Blackett, London, UK, 1925.

KINGSTON Charles	*The Bench And The Dock.*	
		Stanley Paul, London, UK, 1925.

O'DONNELL Elliot	*Confessions Of A Ghost Hunter.*	
		Thornton Butterworth, London, UK, 1928.

O'DONNELL Elliot *Great Thames Mysteries.*
                              Selwyn and Blount, London, UK, 1929.

RICHARDSON   *From City To Fleet Street:*
Joseph Hall   *Some Journalistic Experiences.*
                              Stanley Paul, London, UK, 1927.

LOGAN Guy B.H.   *Masters of Crime: Studies of Multiple Murders.*
                              Stanley Paul, London, UK, 1928.

                  **Includes Chapter 1 – 'The Ripper Murders: New Light
                  on Old Mystery'.**

DOUTHWAITE   *Mass Murder.*
Louis C.   John Long, London, UK, 1928.

DILNOT George   *Scotland Yard: It's History and Organisation*
                  1829 - 1929.
                              Bles, London, UK, 1929.

MOYLAN John   *Scotland Yard And The Metropolitan Police.*
                              Putnam, London, UK, 1929.

MAY Betty   *Tiger Woman: My Story.*
                              Duckworth, London, UK, 1929.

ADAM   *Trial of George Chapman.*
Hargrave Lee   William Hodge, Edinburgh & London,
                              1930.
                              AlsoToronto Law Books, Canada,
                              1930.

BARTON Margaret
SITWELL Osbert

Sober Truth: A Collection of Nineteenth Century
Episodes, Fantastic, Grotesque And Mysterious.
Duckworth, London, UK, 1930.
Reprinted 1944.
Frederick Stokes, New York, USA, 1930.

Includes Chapter 41 - Jack the Ripper.

WENSLEY
Frederick Porter

Forty Years Of Scotland Yard: The Record of A
Lifetime's Service In The Criminal Investigation
Department.
Garden City Publishing, New York, USA, 1930
Reprinted 1933.
Published as *Detective Days.*
Cassell, London, UK, 1931.

NEIL Arthur Fowler

Forty Years of Man-Hunting.
Jarrolds, London, UK, 1932.
Published in America as:
Man Hunters of Scotland Yard.
Doubleday Doran, New York, USA, 1932.

BORCHARD Edwin

Convicting The Innocent: Errors Of Criminal Justice.
Yale University Press, Connecticut, USA, 1932.

Includes a chapter on Frenchy (Ameer Ben Ali) a Ripper
suspect.

WALBROOK H.M.

Murders and Murder Trials 1812 - 1912.
Constable, London, USA, 1932.

Includes a chapter on Jack the Ripper

LEESON Ben
Ex Detective Sergeant

Lost London: The Memoirs of an East End Detective.
Stanley Paul, London, Not Dated (circa 1934).

WOODHALL
Edwin T.

Crime And The Supernatural.
John Long, London, UK, 1935.

Chapter IV includes a look at the Ripper.

HOPKINS
R. Thurston

Life And Death At The Old Bailey.
Herbert Jenkins, London, UK, 1935.

ALAN A.J.
and Others

Great Unsolved Crimes.
Hutchinson & Co., London, UK, 1935.
Hyperion, New York, USA, 1975.

Includes a chapter 'Who Was Jack the Ripper?' by Doctor Harold Dearden.

THOMSON Basil

The Story of Scotland Yard.
Grayson, London, UK, 1935.

PARRISH J.M.
CROSSLAND
John R (Editors)

The Fifty Most Amazing Crimes Of The Last 100 Years.
Odhams Press Ltd., London, UK, 1936.

Includes 'The Fiend Of East London: Jack the Ripper'. By F.A. Beaumont.

PEARSON
Edmund

More Studies In Murder.
Random House, New York, USA, 1936.
Reprinted Arco Publications, London, UK, 1953.

DEW Walter   *I Caught Crippen.*
                                        Blackie & Son Ltd., London & Glasgow,
                                        1938.

                         **One third of the book is devoted to the case under the
                         heading "My Hunt For Jack the Ripper".**

WILLIAMS Watkin   *The Life of General Sir Charles Warren.*
                                        Basil Blackwell, Oxford, UK, 1941.

ODDIE S. Ingleby   *Inquest.*
                                        Hutchinson & Co., London, UK, 1941.

                         Chapter IV includes 'The Ripper and Other Murders'

BELLOC   *The Merry Wives of Westminster.*
LOWNDES   MacMillan, London, UK, 1946.
Mrs. Marie

                         **The third chapter contains an explanation on the origins
                         of her famous novel 'The Lodger'.**

MOORE-
ANDERSON A.P.   *Sir Robert Anderson and Lady Agnes Anderson.*
                                        Marshall, Morgan & Scott Ltd.,
                                        London, UK, 1947.

BARKER Richard   *The Fatal Caress and Other Accounts of*
(Editor)   *English Murders From 1551 to 1888.*
                                        Duell,Sloane & Pearce, New York,
                                        USA, 1947
                                        Dell Books, New York, USA, 1947, P/B
                                        (No. 733)

                         **Includes -' The Jack the Ripper murders 1888 from The
                         London Times'.**

BROCK Alan   *A Casebook of Crime.*
                                         Rockliff, London, 1948

              Includes a chapter titled 'Jack the Ripper'.

O'DONNELL Elliot   *Haunted Britain.*
                                         Rider, London, UK, 1948.

BINNEY Cecil   *Crime and Abnormality.*
                                         Oxford University Press, Oxford, UK,
                                         1948.

SITWELL Osbert   *Noble Essences of Courteous Revelations.*
                                         MacMillan, London, UK, 1950.

HOPKINS   *The World's Strangest Ghost Stories.*
R. Thurston   The World's Work Ltd., Surrey, UK,
                                         1955.
                                         Cedar Books (No. 57), Surrey, UK,
                                         1958, P/B.

              Includes chapter XIX 'Jack the Ripper and Witchcraft'.

LAMPITT L.F.   *World's Strangest Stories.*
                                         Associated Newspapers Ltd., London,
                                         UK, 1955.
                                         Cox Books, London, UK, 1975, P/B.

              **Includes a chapter on Jack the Ripper where Bill
              McGowran offers eight possible solutions to the mystery.**

COBB Belton   *Critical Years At The Yard: The Career of*
Frederick Williamson Of The Detective
Department And The C.I.D.
Faber and Faber, London, UK,
1956.

AMBLER Eric   *The Ability To Kill: And Other Pieces.*
The Curtis Publishing Co., 1956.
Bodley Head Ltd., London, UK, 1963.
Four Square, London, UK, 1964, P/B.
Reprinted 1965.
New English Library, London, 1970,
P/B.

**The Ripper is discussed in a chapter titled 'Criminal
London'.**

BROWNE   *The Rise of Scotland Yard:*
Douglas G   *A History of The Metropolitan Police.*
George Harrap & Co., London, UK,
1956.
Putnam, New York, USA, 1956.

SEARCH Pamela   *Great True Crime Stories - Men.*
(Editor)   Arco Publications Ltd., London, UK,
1957.

**Includes Chapter VII "The Mystery of Jack the Ripper" ˙
by Leonard Matters. According to Melvin Harris this
account was actually written by Alan Hynd.**

HYND Alan   *Sleuths, Slayers, and Swindlers –*
A Casebook of Crime.
Barnes & Noble, New York, USA,
1959.

**The Ripper case is discussed in a chapter entitled "The
Case of the Compulsive Killer".**

HALSTED D.G.   *Doctor In The Nineties.*
                                        Christopher Johnson, London, UK,
                                        1959.

                   Includes Chapter 3 "Jack the Ripper".

SPENCER SHEW   *A Companion To Murder.*
Edward   Cassell & Co., London, UK, 1960.
                                        Knopf, New York, USA, 1962.

WILSON Colin and *Encyclopaedia of Murder.*
PITMAN Patricia   Arthur Barker, London, UK, 1961
                                        Pan Books, London, UK, 1964, P/B
                                        and 1984 P/B.

DAVIDSON Avram   *Crimes and Chaos.*
                                        Regency Books, Evanston, Illinois,
                                        USA, 1962, P/B.

                   **Includes a chapter on The Ripper entitled "Midwife to
                   Murder".**

HARRISON Michael *London By Gaslight 1861 -1911.*
                                        Peter Davies. London, UK, 1963.
                                        Revised Gasogene, Iowa, USA, 1987.

JANNINO E.A.   *Jack the Ripper.*

                   **A paper presented to a discussion session at the 3ʳᵈ
                   International meeting on Forensic Pathology in London
                   in 1963.**

MASTERS R.E.L.   *Sex Crimes In History.*
LEA Eduard   Julian Press, New York, USA, 1963.

50

CARGILL David and
HOLLAND Julian
    Scenes of Murder: A London Guide.
           Heinemann, London, UK, 1964.

An exceedingly rare book which was withdrawn by the publisher.

SCOTT Sir Harold · *The Concise Encyclopaedia of Crime and Criminals.*
           Deutsch, London, UK, 1961.
           Bookplan, London, UK, 1965.

The Ripper entry is though to have been penned by Donald McCormick.

MINTO G.A.
    The Thin Blue Line.
           Hodder & Stoughton, London, UK,
           1965.

FRANKLIN Charles
    The World's Worst Murderers.
    Exciting and Authentic Accounts of the
    Great Classics of Murder.
           Odhams Books Ltd., London, UK,
           1965
           Taplinger, New York, USA, 1965.

Chapter 1 "Human Butchers" takes a look at the Ripper case.

BROPHY John
    The Meaning of Murder.
           Whiting Books, London, UK, 1966.
           Corgi Books, London, UK, P/B.

SYMONS Julian
    Crime and Detection. An Illustrated History
    from 1840.
           Studio Vista, London, UK, 1966.
           Released in America as *"A Pictorial*
           History of Crime".
           Crown Publishing, New York, USA,
           1966.

MORLAND Nigel   *An Outline of Sexual Criminology.*
                           Tallis Books, Oxford, UK, 1966, P/B.

NO LISTED   *The Left Handed Book.*
AUTHOR   Souvenir Press, London, UK, 1966.

Contains "Left Handed Jack".

CAMPS Francis and   *The Investigation of Murder.*
BARBER Richard   Michael Joseph Ltd., London, UK,
                           1966.
                           Scientific Book Club Edition, London,
                           1966

MACKLIN John   *The Enigma of The Unknown.*
                           Ace Books, New York USA, 1967,
                           P/B.

Includes a chapter entitled "Jack the Ripper Mystery - Solved In A Dream".

GRIBBLE Leonard   *They Had A Way With Women.*
                           John Long, London, UK, 1967.

Contains "The Beast With the Knife".

EHRLICH Blake   *London On The Thames.*
                           Cassell & Co., London, UK, 1968.

PEARSALL Ronald   *The Worm In The Bud: The World of*
                     Victorian Sexuality.
                           Weidenfeld & Nicolson, London, UK,
                           1969

WILSON Colin	*A Casebook Of Murder.* Frewin, London, UK, 1969. Cowles, New York, USA, 1970.

ARCHER Fred | *Crime And The Psychic World.*
W. Morrow, New York, USA, 1969.
Reprinted in UK as *"Ghost Detectives".*
W.H. Allen, London, UK, 1970.

Includes "Human Bloodhound Tracked Jack the Ripper".

ALTICK Richard | *Victorian Studies in Scarlet.*
W.W. Norton, New York, USA, 1970.
Jim Dent, London, UK, 1972.

SQUIRE Robin | *Classic Murders.*

Foulsham, London, UK, 1970

GOODMAN Jonathan | *Bloody Versicles: The Rhymes of Crime.*
David and Charles, Newton Abbot, UK, 1971.
St. Martin's Press, New York, USA, 1971.
Kent State University Press, Ohio, USA, 1993 P/B.

WILLIAMS Guy | *The Hidden World of Scotland Yard.*
Hutchinson, London, UK, 1972.

BAVERSTOCK Keith | *Footsteps Through London's Past.*
Aylesbury, Bucks, UK, 19712.

PLATNICK Kenneth   *Great Mysteries of History.*
>David and Charles, Newton Abbot, UK, 1972.

Includes a chapter "Yours Truly Jack the Ripper: The Scourge of London's East End".

SPARROW Gerald   *Crimes of Passion.*
>Arthur Barker Ltd., London, UK, 1973.

Includes a chapter on the Ripper entitled "Was it The Duke of Clarence?".

BUTLER Ivan   *Murderer's London.*
>Robert Hale, London, UK, 1973
>Robert Hale, London, UK, 1992, P/B.

Includes a chapter called "The Ripper's Streets".

DOWNIE R. Angus   *Murder In London: A Topographical Guide To Famous Crimes.*
>Arthur Barker Ltd., London, UK, 1973.

In the chapter "Towards The East" the author looks at the Ripper murders.

HARRISON Michael   *The World of Sherlock Holmes.*
>Frederick Muller Ltd., London, UK, 1973.
>New English Library, London, UK, 1975, P/B.
>Dutton, New York, USA, 1975.

Includes a chapter on the crimes entitled "The Ripper and The Crown".

CAMPS Francis   *Camps On Crime.*
David & Charles, Newton Abbot, UK, 1973.

Includes the chapter "More About Jack the Ripper".

ACKROYD Peter   *Evil London.*
Wolfe Publishing, London, UK, 1973.

DE VRIES Leonard   *Horrible Murder: Victorian Crime and Passion.*
London, UK, 1974.

VISICK Jacquelyn   *London Tales of Terror.*
Fontana Books, London, UK, 1972.
Reprinted 1974 and 1975 P/B.

MCCONNELL Brian   *Found Naked And Dead.*
New English Library, London, UK, 1974.
New English Library, London, UK, 1975 P/B.

A series of murders to rival that of Jack the Ripper. Set in London in the 1950's and 1960's a killer known as Jack the Stripper is at large. Based on a true series of murders.

NO LISTED
AUTHOR   *The Readers Digest Book of Strange Stories and Amazing Facts.*
Readers Digest, London, UK, 1975.

JACKSON Robert   *Francis Camps: Famous Case Histories of the*
                     Celebrated Pathologist.
                                     Hart, Davis, MacGibbon Ltd., London,
                                     UK, 1975.

                     Includes chapter 9 "Camps on Jack the Ripper".

FISHMAN William   *East End Jewish Radicals 1875-1914.*
                                     Duckworth, London, UK, 1975.

LUSTGARTEN Edgar   *The Illustrated Story of Crime.*
                                     Weidenfeld & Nicolson, London, UK,
                                     1976.
                                     Follet, Chicago, USA, 1976.

ANON   *Crimes and Punishments: A Pictorial*
                     Encyclopaedia of Aberrant Behaviour.
                                     B.P.C. Publishing, New York, USA,
                                     1974. (20 volumes).

HARRISON Fraser   *The Dark Angel: Aspects of Victorian Sexuality.*
                                     Sheldon Press, London, UK, 1977.

GREX Leo   *Detection Stranger Than Fiction.*
                                     Robert Hale Ltd., London, UK, 1977.

                     **Chapter entitled "The Man Who Wasn't Jack the
                     Ripper".**

FARSON Daniel   *The Hamlyn Book of Horror.*
                                     Hamlyn Publishing, London, UK, 1979.
                                     Originally published as:
                                     The Beaver Book of Horror.
                                     Hamlyn Publishing, London, UK, 1977,
                                     P/B.

BOROWITZ Albert	*Innocence and Arsenic.*	
		Harper & Row, New York, USA, 1977.

HUGHES Mary Vivien	*A London Girl In The 1880's*	
		Oxford University Press, Oxford, UK, 1978, P/B.

ALEXANDER Marc   *Royal Murder.*

Frederick Muller,London,UK,1978.

Includes "Royalty and the Ripper" by Colin Wilson.

MADISON Arnold   *Great Unsolved Cases.*

Franklin Watts, New York, USA, 1978.
Dell Books, New York, USA, 1980, P/B.

Includes Chapter Two - "Jack the Ripper".

MUMFORD
Prudence   *Famous Names In Crime.*

Wayland Press, England, 1978.

Contains "Jack the Ripper: The Terror of London".

GAUTE Joseph
ODELL Robin &   *The Murderers Who's Who.*

George Harrap, London, UK, 1979.

WAGNER
Gillian   *Barnardo.*

Weidenfeld & Nicolson, London, UK, 1979.

MOORE James &
DAHL Norman
Crime and Justice: From Cain to Crippen.
Hamlyn Publishing, London, UK, 1980.
Scholastic Press, London, UK, 1980,
P/B.

MAY Robin
*The Quiz Book Of Crime: Hundreds of Questions From
Capone To Crippen - Jack the Ripper To Burke And Hare.*
Futura, London, UK, 1980, Paperback.

**A quiz book which has 16 questions on Jack the Ripper in
chapter 25.**

BLUNDELL Nigel
The World's Greatest Mysteries.
Octopus Books, London, UK, 1980.
Berkley Books, New York, USA,
1988.

WHITE Jerry
*Rothchild Building - Life In An East End Tenement Building
1887 - 1920.*
Routledge, Kegan, Paul Ltd., London,
UK, 1980.

GREEN Jonathon
A Directory of Infamy: The Best of The Worst.
Mills & Boon, London, UK, 1980.

MARNE Patricia
Crime and Sex in Handwriting.
Constable, London, UK, 1981.

HAINES Max
Crime Flashback - Book 2.
Toronto Sun, Canada, 1981.

GUATE Joe &
ODELL Robin
Murder Whatdunit.
Harrap, London, UK, 1982.

BROOKS J.A.   *Ghosts of London - The East End, City and North.*
                                              London 1982.

HONEYCOMBE   *The Murders of the Black Museum 1870-1970.*
Gordon   Hutchinson, London, UK, 1982.

NASH Jay Robert   *Compendium of World Crime.*
                                              Harrap, London, UK, 1983.

WILSON Colin   *A Criminal History of Mankind.*
                                              Granada, London, UK, 1984.

FRIEDLAND   *The Trials of Israel Lipski.*
Martin   MacMillan , London, UK, 1984.
                                              Beaufort Books, New York, USA,
                                              1984.

BOAR Roger &   *The World's Most Infamous Murders.*
BLUNDELL Nigel   Octopus Books, London, UK, 1983.
                                              Octopus Books, London, UK, 1984,
                                              P/B.

CHAPMAN Pauline   *Madame Tussauds Chamber of Horrors.*
                                              Constable, London, UK, 1984.
                                              Grafton Books, London, UK, 1985,
                                              P/B.

NOGUCHI Thomas   *Coroner At Large.*
                                              Simon & Schuster, New York, USA,
                                              1985.

          Includes a chapter entitled "Who Was Jack the Ripper?".

GAUTE Joe   *Murder Whereabouts.*
ODELL Robin   Harrap, London, UK, 1986.

PORTER Roy &   *Rape.*
TOMASELLI Sylvana   Blackwell, Oxford, UK, 1986.

Includes an excellent chapter by Professor Christopher Frayling entitled "The House That Jack Built – Some Stereotypes Of The Rapist In The History Of Popular Culture".

CAMERON Deborah & *The Lust To Kill.*
FRAZER Eizabeth   Polity Press, Cambridge, UK, 1987.
                         New York University Press, New York, USA, 1987.

CAPUTI Jane   *The Age of Sex Crime.*
                         The Women's Press Ltd., London, UK, 1988.
                         Ohio Bowling Green University Press, Ohio, USA, 1987.

Includes Chapter 1 - "The Ripper Repository". Chapter 2 - "The Ripper Repetitions".

GLYN-JONES   *Unsolved: Classic True Murder Cases.*
Richard   Xanadu Publications Ltd., London, UK, 1987.
                         Guild Book Club Edition, London, UK, 1987.
                         Star Books, London, UK, 1988, P/B.

Includes "My Search For Jack the Ripper" by Colin Wilson.

FIDO Martin	*Murder Guide to London.* Grafton Books, London, UK, 1987.
BLOOM Clive & DOCHERTY Brian & GIBB Jane & SHAND Keith	*Nineteenth Century Mystery and Suspense:* *From Poe to Conan Doyle.* MacMillan, Hampshire, UK, 1988.

Includes "The House That Jack Built: Jack the Ripper, Legend and The Power of the Unknown" by Clive Bloom.

NEWTON Michael	*Mass Murder: An Annotated Bibliography.* Garland, New York, USA, 1988.
HARLEY LEWIS Roy	*Victorian Murders.* David & Charles, Newton Abbot, UK,1988.
WHITTINGTON- EGAN Richard & Molly	*The Bedside Book of Murder.* David & Charles, Newton Abbot, UK, 1988.
LANE Brian	*The Murder Club Guide to Great Britain.* Harrap, London, UK, 1988. Retitled *The Murder Guide to Great Britain:* *100 Bizarre and Gruesome Murders.* Robinson Publishing Ltd., London, UK, 1993.
PRINCE Michael	*Murderous Places.* Blandford Press, London, UK, 1989.

CANNING John   *Unsolved Murders and Mysteries.*
Chancellor Press, London, UK, 1989.
Futura Books, London, UK, 1991, P/B.
Chancellor Press, London, UK, 1993, P/B.

ANON   *Infamous Crimes That Shocked The World.*
Caxton, London, UK, 1989.

Includes "Who Was Jack the Ripper?" and "The Ripper's Reign of Terror". Both originally appeared in 'Crime and Punishment Magazine' 1973.

BLUNDELL Nigel   *World's Greatest Unsolved Crimes.*
Berkley Books, New York, USA, 1990.
Hamlyn Books, London, U.K., 1994.

WILSON Colin   *The Mammoth Book of True Crime 2.*
Robinson Publishing, London, U.K., 1990.

Includes Chapter Nine "The Ripper Mystery".

ROBINSON John   *Born In Blood.*
Century Books, London, U.K., 1990.
Arrow Books, London, U.K., 1993, P/B.

SOLOMAN Philip   *Ghosts, Legends and Psychic Snippets.*
P.K.N. Publications, West Midlands, UK., 1990, P/B-Booklet.

Includes Chapter Ten "Was Jack the Ripper Caught By A Victorian Medium?".

WINTER Gordon &   *Secrets Of The Royals.*
KOCHMAN Wendy   Robson Books, London, U.K., 1990.

COSTELLO Peter   *The Real World of Sherlock Holmes.*
                                     Caroll & Graf, New York, USA, 1991.
                                     Robinson, London, U.K., 1991.

YARWOOD Derek   *Outrages, Fatal And Other.*
                        A Chronicle Of Cheshire Crime 1612 –1912.
                                     Didsbury Press, Manchester, 1991,
                                     P/B.

Chapter 10 – "Bessie: Bride of Jack the Ripper", Lists George Chapman as a probable suspect. The book itself is blessed with a Jack the Ripper cover.

JEFFERS H. Paul   *Bloody Business: An Anecdotal History of Scotland Yard.*
                                     Pharos Books, New York, USA,
                                     1992.

Includes a look at The Ripper in Chapter Seven - "Saucy Jack".

WELLER Philip with   *The Life And Times of Sherlock Holmes.*
RODEN Christopher   Studio Editions, London, U.K., 1992.
                                     Bracken Books, London, U.K., 1992.
                                     Crescent Books, New York & New
                                     Jersey, USA, 1992.

Includes the Chapter "A Scholarly Case Study: The Problem of Sherlock Holmes and Jack the Ripper.

WALKOWITZ
Judith
City of Dreadful Delight; Narratives of Sexual Danger In Late-Victorian London.
Virago Press, London, U.K., 1992.
University of Chicago Press, Chicago,USA, 1992.

Chapter Seven entitled "Jack the Ripper".

WILSON Colin
World Famous Gaslight Murders.
Magpie Books Ltd., London, U.K., 1992. P/B.

BEGG Paul &
SKINNER Keith
The Scotland Yard Files: 150 Years of The C.I.D.
Headline Books, London, U.K., 1992.

PRINCE Theodore
Hitchcock And Homosexuality: His Fifty Year Obsession With Jack the Ripper And The Superbitch Prostitute: A Psychoanalytical Review.
Scarecrow Press, Maryland, USA., 1992.

BYRNE Richard
The London Dungeon Book of Crime and Punishment.
Little Brown, London, U.K., 1993.

McCARTY John
Movie Psychos And Madness.
Citadel Press, England, 1993.

Chapter Two is devoted to the legend of The Ripper and the films he inspired.

WADDELL Bill
The Black Museum: New Scotland Yard.
Little Brown, London, U.K., 1993.

CANTER David | *Criminal Shadows - Inside The Mind Of A Serial Killer.*
> Harper Collins, London, U.K., 1994.
> Harper Collins, London, U.K., 1995, P/B.

ARONSON Theo | *Prince Eddy and The Homosexual Underworld.*
> John Murray Ltd., London, U.K., 1994.
> John Murray Ltd., London, U.K., 1996, P/B.
> Barnes & Noble, New York, USA., 1995.

WHITTINGTON-EGAN Molly | *Scottish Murder Stories.*
> Neil Wilson Publishing, Glasgow, U.K., 1998.

Includes a chapter - "Jock the Ripper" based on William Henry Bury.

WILKES Roger | *The Mammoth Book Of Unsolved Crime.*
> Robinson Publishing, London, UK, 1999, P/B.

Includes a chapter "Jack the Ripper: The Whitechapel Murders 1888" by Philip Sugden.

GRAYSMITH Robert | *The Bell Tower: The Case Of Jack The Ripper Finally Solved In San Francisco.*
> Regnery Publishing, Washington, USA, 1999.

FOREIGN LANGUAGE PUBLICATIONS.

LACASSAGNE
Jean Aleandre

Vacher L'Eventreur Et Les Crimes Sadiques.
Masson, Paris, France, 1899.

Includes photographs of the Kelly and Eddowes corpses and reports of the murders.

DYBWAD Vilhelm
(Editor)

Skyldug Eller Ikke Skyldug.
Gyldendal, Norway, 1934.

Translates as "Guilty Or Not Guilty" and has a chapter "Who Was Jack the Ripper?".

ALLEN William

Morderen Der Aldrig Blev Fanget - Og Maske Fanget.
Denmark, 1938.

William Allen is a pseudonym of Richard Jeuseu and the title translates as "The Murderer That Was Never Caught - and Maybe Caught".
It is unclear if this book is dedicated to Jack the Ripper or just contains a report on the murders. The Royal Danish Library, which claims to own a copy of every book published in Denmark, has no record of this book's existence - but I have it on very good authority that it does indeed exist.

NO LISTED
AUTHOR

Archives du Crime No. IV: 13 Grands Tueurs
Amiot-Dumont, Paris, France, 1948.

A true crime study which includes the chapter "*La Sinistre Enigme de Jack L'Eventreur.*"

EGER Rudolf

Beruhmte Kriminalfalle Aus Vier Jahrhunderten.
Albert Nauck & Co., Germany, 1949.

Carries a fifteen page report on the murders.

DI BELLA Franco   *Il Museo Dei Sanguinari.*
Sugar Editore, Milan, Italy, 1962

Chapter VII - Jack Lo Sventratore.

OLSSON Jan   Olof *Generalelr Och Likstallda.*
Stockholm. Sweden, 1970.

Includes Tom Cullen's account of the murders.

FUCHS J.M.   *Moord Op Alfabet.*
SIMONS W.J.   Uitgeverij B.V., Amsterdam, Holland,
1974.

Includes Jack the Ripper in this alphabet of world famous murders.

ASFOUR   *Meutres Par Procuration - Les Assassins*
Jean Claude   *a L'Ecran.*
Editions P.A.C., Paris, France, 1979.

MYSTFEST CATOLOGUE 1988.

Catalogue of the ninth festival of Mystery writers held in Italy in 1988. Includes a detailed look at the Ripper case by Ripper experts including - Stephane Bourgoin; Daniel Farson and Donald Rumbelow.

BOURGOIN   *Jack L'Eventreur: Centenaire D'un Mystere.*
Stephane
FIDO Martin and
BEGG Paul

Catalogue of the tenth Festival du Poplar, held in Grenoble, France, 1988.

VERGES Jacques   *Les Sanguinaires Mystere Du Crime.*
                                Michael Lafon, Paris, France, 1992.

Includes "Jack L'Eventreur: Un Tueur en Quete D'Identite.

GOENS Jean   *Loups-Garous, Vampires et Autres Monstres.*
                                CNRS Editions, Paris, France, 1993.

Chapter five - "L'affaire Jack L'Eventreur.

BOURGOIN   *Serial Killers.*
Stephane   Grasset, Paris, France, 1993.

BENEZECH Michel   *La Chair De L'Ame: 50 Essais Sur La Medecine.*
                                Editions Privee, Bordeaux, France, 1994.

Includes "Jack the Ripper Ou de la Mutilation Voluptueuse.

BOURGOIN   *Crimes et Faits Divers.*
Stephane   Editions Mereal, Paris, France, 1997.

Includes "Jack the Ripper".

FOUR.

JACK THE RIPPER IN FICTION.

Ever since the Ripper put down his knife, the flow of fictional material published has been constant.

The case certainly seems to grow in popularity each year and Jack the Ripper has featured in novels, short stories, plays and poems on both sides of the Atlantic. The Ripper case seems to have been covered from every angle although I'm sure that in the future we will continue to see the Ripper take part in time travel and be pursued by Sherlock Holmes and Doctor Watson, as they have done so, so many times in the past, both of whom have been named as the Whitechapel Murderer in fictional works.

As you will see in the Foreign Language section, France has been responsible for a fair number of Ripper novels being published. Maybe one day we will see them translated into English.

BREWER John Francis	*The Curse Upon Mitre Square AD 1530 - 1888.* Simpkin Marshall, London, UK, 1888. J.W. Lovell, New York, USA, 1889.
DETECTIVE WARREN	*The Whitechapel Murders: or On The Track of The Fiend.* Old Cap Collier Library Series No. 333; Munro's Publishing House, New York, USA, 31st December 1888. Reprinted by The Ripperological Preservation Society, Paramus, New Jersey, USA, 1998.
RODISSI (pseudonym Jacob Ringgold).	*Lord Jacquelin Burkney: The Whitechapel Terror.* Anton Publishing Co., USA, January 15th 1889. Due to be reprinted in 1999 by The Ripperological Preservation Society, Paramus, New Jersey, USA.
PINKERTON A.F.	*The Whitechapel Murders: or An American Detective in London.* The Pinkerton Detective Series, Laird and Lee Publishers, Chicago, USA, No. 21, Nov. 1889. Reprinted by The Ripperological Preservation Society, Paramus, New Jersey, USA, 1996.
JEROME Gilbert	*Jack the Ripper: or The Whitechapel Fiend in America.* Old Cap Collier Library Series No. 338, Munro's Publishing House, New York, USA, 18th February 1889. Reprinted by The Ripperological Preservation Society, Paramus, New Jersey, USA, 1996.

LAWSON W.B.   *Jack the Ripper in New York: or Piping a*
                          Terrible Mystery.
                                        Log Cabin Library Series, Street and
                                        Smith Publishing, New York, USA,
                                        1891.

                          **Reprinted by The Ripperological Preservation Society,
                          Paramus, New Jersey, USA, 1996.**

OLIVER N.T.   *The Whitechapel Mystery: Jack the Ripper -*
                          A Psychological Problem.
                                        Globe Detective Series, No. 14.
                                        Continental Publishing, Chicago Eagle,
                                        1889.
                                        Chicago Patrol Volume 1, No. 8, 1891.

LAW John   *In Darkest London.*
                                        Reeves, London, UK, 1891.

MURPHY G. Read   *The Blakely Tragedy: 1892.*

                          A novel based on Jack the Ripper.

ROSE F.W.   *I Will Repay.*
                                        Eden, Remington & Co., 1892.

                          A novel based on Jack the Ripper.

BELLOC
LOWNDES
Mrs. Marie

The Lodger.

Probably the most famous of all fictional works based on the Whitechapel Murders. Since it was first published it has remained a classic work and has been translated into many languages, as well as being made into films and plays - viewed and performed worldwide.

The work itself first appeared in America in 1911 in McClures Magazine and was an immediate success.

It was first published by Scribner's of New York and has since been reprinted on countless occasions. Millions of copies exist in many different editions and it would be almost impossible to list them all. Most of the best and important editions available are listed below:

Scribner, New York, USA, 1911.

Methuen, London, UK, 1913. (Reprinted seven times before 1926 and for the eighth time in 1949).

Tauchnitz Edition, Volume 4453, Leipzig, 1913, Pocket Edition.

Readers Library Publishing Co. Ltd., London, UK,

March 1927 (150,000 copies); May 1927 (50,000 copies); July 1927 (50,000 copies). Issued with a dustjacket with an illustration showing Ivor Novello.

Longmans, New York, USA, 1940. Issued with a dustjacket with a large eye and Ripper type figure on the cover.

Pocket Books, New York, USA, 1940, paperback (No. 43).

Reprinted 1941 with a different cover.

The World Publishing Co., New York, USA, 1944, in the Tower Mystery series. Issued with a wonderful dustjacket showing Laird Cregar and

Merle Oberon in scenes from the 20th Century Fox motion picture released the previous year.
Pan Books, London, UK, 1947, paperback; reprinted 1950 (No. 17) with a different cover.
Dell Books, New York, USA, 1964 (No. 4903), P/B.
Four Square Books, London, UK, 1966, (No. 1674) P/B.
Hamish Hamilton, London, UK, 1969. A Finger Print book.
Avon Books, New York, USA, 1971, Paperback.
The Franklin Library, Pennsylvania, USA, 1990,
Hardback, not issued with a dustjacket - blue boards with gold lettering - a lovely edition.
Academy Books, New York, USA, 1988, Paperback.
Oxford University Press, Oxford, 1996, Paperback.

ALLEN F.   *Whitechapel Murder.*
                           Ogilvie, USA, Circa 1927.

CENDRARS Blaise   *Moravagine.*
                           Bernard Grassett, France, 1926.
                           Translated - Peter Owen, England, 1968.
                           Penguin Books, London, UK, 1979, P/B.

Part II Chapter Nine - "Jack the Ripper".

BEEDING Francis | *Death Walks in Eastrepps.*
Hodder & Stoughton, London, UK, 1931.
Mystery League Publishers, USA, 1931.
Dover Publishing. USA, 1980, Paperback.

Six murders committed by a killer based on Jack.

BURKE Thomas | *The Pleasantries of Old Quong.*
Constable, London, UK, 1931.
Published in America as - *A Teashop in Limehouse.*
Little Brown, Boston, USA, 1931.

Includes the Ripper short story :The Hands of Mr. Ottermole".

BROOKE Hugh | *Man Made Angry.*
Longmans, London, UK, 1932.
Longmans, New York, USA, 1932.

Based on the Ripper murders.

ARLEN Michael | *Hell Said The Duchess - A Bedtime Story.*
Doubleday, Doran & Co., New York, USA, 1934.
Heinemann Ltd., London, UK, 1934.

It is not Jack, but Jane the Ripper in this fictional account of the crimes.

TYRER Walter *Jane The Ripper.*
        Columbine Publishing, London, UK,
        Circa 1934.

A whole countryside is terrified by a cruel and calculating woman known as Jane the Ripper. Is the killer a man disguised as a woman?

MacDONALD *Bank Holiday On Parnassus.*
LAING Allen   Allen & Unwin, London, UK, 1941.

Contains a "Jack the Ripper" poem.

BLOCH Robert *The Opener Of The Way.*
        Arkham House, Sauk City, USA, 1945.
        Neville Spearman, Jersey, UK, 1968.
        Granada Publishing, London, UK,
        1976, P/B.

Contains "Yours Truly Jack the Ripper". Also appeared in Bloch's *"The House of The Hatchet – A New Collection of Horror Stories".*

        Tandem Books, London, UK, 1965,
        P/B.

Actually published as *"Yours Truly Jack the Ripper".*

        Belmont Books, New York, USA,
        1962.
        Pulphouse Publishing, Oregon, USA,
        1991.
        No. 10 in Short Story Paperback
        Series.

This classic story first appeared in the American magazine "Weird Tales" in July 1943 and sees The Ripper stalk Chicago in the 1940's.

LUSTGARTEN   *A Case To Answer.*
Edgar   Eyre & Spottiswood, London, UK,
                                1947.
                                Reprinted in America as -
                                One More Unfortunate.
                                Charles Scribners, New York, USA,
                                1947.
                                Gregg Press, Boston, USA, 1980.
                                Dell Books, New York, USA, 1955,
                                Paperback, (No. 299).

A tale which sees a disciple of the Ripper carrying out similar crimes.

SKENE Anthony   *The Ripper Returns.*
                                Pemberton, Manchester, UK, 1948.

The Ripper is tracked down by the detective Sexton Blake.

ERSKINE Margaret   *Give Up The Ghost.*
                                Doubleday & Co., New York, USA,
                                1949.
                                Hammond & Co., London, UK, 1949.
                                Ian Henry Publications, Essex, UK,
                                1975.

Continued....

BROWN Fredric *The Screaming Mimi.*

Dutton & Co., New York, USA, 1949.

Boardman, London, UK, 1950.

Bantam Books, London, UK, 1950,

Paperback.

Corgi Books, London, UK, 1958,

Paperback.

Sabre Books, London, UK, 1967,

Paperback.

Caroll & Graff, New York, USA,

1989, P/B.

**A heavy drinking reporter gets involved with a 'Ripper"
who terrorises Chicago - murdering one beautiful girl after
another.**

CAPON Paul *The Seventh Passenger.*

Wardlock, London, UK, 1953.

A story of a killer loosely based on Jack the Ripper.

BARNARD Allan *The Harlot Killer - Jack the Ripper*

(Ed) *In Fact And Fiction.*

Dodd & Mead, New York, USA, 1953.

Dell Books, New York, USA, 1953, P/B

(No.797).

**Of the thirteen short stories contained in this anthology
nine are fictional:**
1. **Donald Henderson - The Alarm Bell.**
2. **William Samson – The Intruder.**
3. **Anthony Boucher - The Stripper.**
4. **Kay Rogers - Love Story.**
5. **Thomas Burke - The Hands of Mr. Ottermole.**
6. **Theodora Benson - In The Fourth Ward.**
7. **Mrs. M. Belloc Lowndes - The Lodger.**
8. **Anon - Jack El Destripador.**
9. **Robert Bloch - Yours Truly Jack the Ripper.**

WILLIAMSON J.N.
WILLIAMS H.B &
(Eds)

Illustrious Clients Third Casebook.
Indianapolis, USA, 1953.

Contains "Sherlock Holmes and Jack the Ripper" by Gordon Neitzke.

BLOCH Robert

The Will To Kill: Was He To Be Jack the Ripper All Over Again?
Ace Books, New York, USA, 1954,
Paperback, (No. 5-67).

A man wonders if he is a modern Jack the Ripper, as he considers himself responsible for a series of shocking murders.

BRECHT Bertolt

The Threepenny Opera.
Metheun, London, UK, 1994,
Paperback.

Originally translated from the German edition "*Die Dreigroschenoper*" (1929) and published in the UK in 1954.

ALEXANDER David

Terror On Broadway.
Random House, New York, USA, 1954.
Boardman, London, UK, 1956.
Bantam Books, New York, USA, 1956,
P/B.

A journalist trails a modern day Jack the Ripper who despises the pretty girls of New York's Great White Way.

DESMOND Hugh   *A Scream In The Night.*
Wright & Brown, London, UK, 1955.

A tale of Jack the Ripper.

DESMOND Hugh   *Death Let Loose.*
Wright & Brown, London, UK, 1956.

A modern day Jack the Ripper who prefers children.

PROCTOR Maurice   *Ripper Murders.*
Avon Books, New York, USA, 1956,
Paperback, (No. 794).
Published in the UK as "*I Will Speak Daggers*".

A Hard-hitting story of two Scotland Yard detectives and a vicious knife killer.

FOX Gardner   *Terror Over London.*
Gold Medal Books, Fawcett
Publications, Connecticut, USA, 1957,
Paperback (No. 648).

A rather scarce book set in London in 1888. Jack the Ripper is on the loose where the very mention of his name strikes fear and horror into the heart of the city. Recommended.

SMITH Edgar W.   *Baker Street And Beyond: Together With Semi-Trifling Monographs.*
Baker Street Irregulars, New Jersey,
USA, 1957.

Includes "*The Suppressed Adventures of The Worst Man in London*".

JAMES Stuart   *Jack the Ripper.*
                                Frederick Fell, New York, USA, 1959.
                                Monarch Books, Connecticut, USA,
                                1960, Paperback, (No. 143).
                                Horrowitz, Sydney, Australia, 1960 and
                                1962, Paperbacks.

**A novel based on the Joseph E. Levine motion picture
starring Eddie Byrne, released in 1958. The book also
contains a 'true to life' account of the Ripper murders by
Bill Doll, however the Australian edition does not.**

JOHNSON Ames   *Leaves From The Copper Beeches.*
HART Thomas   Livingston Publishing Co., Narberth,
SHALET Henry A.   USA, 1959.
STARR H.W. (Eds)   Contains:
                               Charles Fisher - A Challenge from
                               Baker Street.
                               Charles Fisher - Sherlock Holmes and
                               Jack the Ripper.

VAN HELLE}   *Nightmare.*
Marcus   Ophelia Press, Paris, France, 1960,
                               Paperback, (written in English).
                               Brandon House Books, Hollywood,
                               California, USA, 1967, Paperback, (No.
                               2042).

**A novel in which a modern day Jack the Ripper – known
as 'Nightmare' - stalks the terror filled streets.**

WILSON Colin   *Ritual In The Dark.*

Gollancz Ltd., London, UK, 1960.
Houghton & Mifflin, New York, USA,
1960.
Popular Library Edition, New York,
USA, 1961, Paperback, (No. SP85).
Pan Books, London, UK, 1962,
Paperback, (No. M16).
Reprinted 1962, different cover (No.
T50).
Panther Books Ltd., London, UK, 1976,
P/B.
Reprinted 1978, different cover.
Cedric Chivers, Bath, UK, for The
Library Association, 1974, (new
dustjacket).

**A modern day Ripper on the loose in contemporary
London.**

VEHEYNE Cherry   *Horror.*

Digit Books, London, UK, 1965, P/B
(No.R553)
Digit Books, London, UK, 1964, reprint
paperback (different cover) (No. R822).
Published in Australia as *"Jack the
Ripper".*
Bill Ewington Books, Sydney,
Australia, Paperback (not dated).

**An excellent novel set in 1888 London featuring the actual·
victims of Jack.   Difficult to obtain although well worth
tracking down.**

BARING-GOULD *Sherlock Holmes of Baker Street: A Life Of*
William S.   *The World's First Consulting Detective.*
          Hart Davis, London, UK, 1962.
          Wing Books, New Jersey, USA, 1995.

Includes Chapter XV "Jack The Harlot Killer: Friday 9 November - Sunday 11 November 1888".

BEAUMONT Charles *The Fiend In You.*
(Ed)   Ballantine Books, New York,
          USA, 1962.

Includes "A Punishment To Fit The Crimes" by Richard Gordon.

KILPATRICK   *The Mother of Jack the Ripper: A Drama.*
John A.   Samuel French, New York, USA, 1963.

BENEDICT   *Tales of Terror and Suspense.*
Stewart H   Dell Books, New York, USA, 1963,
          Paperback, (No. 8466).

Includes the short story "The Lodger" by Mrs. Marie Belloc Lowndes.

HITCHCOCK Alfred *Sixteen Skeletons In My Closet.*
          Dell Books, New York, USA, 1963,
          Paperback, (No. 8011), reprinted 1964
          and 1973.

Includes the short story "Said Jack the Ripper" by Robert Arthur.

McSHANE Mark   *Untimely Ripped.*
                                    Cassell & Co., London, UK, 1963.
                                    Fawcett Crest Books, New York, 1956,
                                    P/B.

A story of a killer inspired by Jack the Ripper.

WARNER   Douglas *Death of a Tom.*
                                    Cassell & Co., London, UK, 1963.
                                    Corgi Books, London, UK, 1964,
                                    Paperback (No. GC7022).

A novel which features a modern day Ripper killing prostitutes in London.

CUMBERLAND   *Hate Will Find A Way.*
Marten   Hutchinson, London, UK, 1964.

A Saturnin Dax detective novel (No. 32) where an actress is plagued by a killer who signs his letters 'Jack the Riper'.

VAN THAL   *The Fourth Pan Book of Horror Stories.*
Herbert (Ed).   Pan Books, London, UK, 1963, P/B,
                                    (No. 261).
                                    Reprinted by Pan Books continually.

Contains "Dulcie" by Hugh Reid.

TAPPER Oscar   *Jack the Knife.*

> East London Arts Magazine, London,
> 1964.
> Reprinted 1965 and 1970.

A play featuring the Ripper which was first performed at the Toynbee Theatre, Commercial Street, London on 14th April 1965. The book was illustrated by Jimmy Johns and the photographs published were taken by Gordon Stevens. A difficult to find publication.

QUEEN Ellery   *A Study In Terror.*

> Lancer Books, New York, USA, 1966,
> Paperback, (No.73469).
> Lodestone Books, New York, USA,
> 1966, Paperback, (No. B5020).
> Lancer Books, New York, USA, 1967,
> Paperback, (No. 73616).
> Lancer Books, New York, USA, 1969,
> Paperback, (No. 73814).
> Xanadu Publications, London, UK,
> 1991, Paperback.
> Also published in the UK as: *Sherlock Holmes versus Jack the Ripper.*
> Gollancz, London, UK, 1967,
> Hardback.

All five paperback editions had different covers. A novel where the detective Ellery Queen and Sherlock Holmes match wits to reveal the identity of the world's most infamous killer - Jack the Ripper. The film was released in 1965 by Columbia Pictures with John Neville starring as Holmes.

BUCHWALD Art   *Son Of The Great Society.*

> Weidenfeld & Nicolson, London, UK,
> 1967. Chapter IV includes "The Trial
> of Jack the Ripper".

RUSSELL Ray   *Unholy Trinity.*
                                        Bantam, New York, USA, 1967.
                                        Sphere Books, London, UK, 1971,
                                        Paperback, Reprinted 1980.

                      Includes 'Sagittarius' featuring the Ripper.

ELLISON Harlan   *Dangerous Visions.*
                                        Doubleday & Co., New York, USA,
                                        1967.
                                        Bruce & Watson, London, UK, 1970.

                      Includes two Ripper short stories.
                      i)   Robert Bloch - A Toy for Juliette.
                      ii)   Harlan Ellison - The Prowler In The City At
                      The Edge Of The World.
                      (This was also printed in Richard Glyn Jones -
                      Solved - Famous Mystery Writers On Classic
                      True Crime Case. Xanadu, London, UK, 1987.

FARMER Philip Jose   *A Feast Unknown.*
                                        Essex House, New York, USA, 1969.
                                        Quartet Press, London, UK, 1975,
                                        Paperback.
                                        Playboy Press, New York, USA 1980,
                                        Paperback.

                      A novel featuring the legendary Apeman, Lord of the
                      Jungle who is also the son of Jack the Ripper.

GARDNER Michael   *An Old Drama: Three Encounters With*
                      Jack the Ripper.
                                        Black Knight Press, Leicester, UK,
                                        1969.
                                        Limited to 100 copies only.

                      A rather short and scarce look at the world of the Ripper.
                      Beautifully illustrated by Deirdre Maton.

BARNES Peter   *The Ruling Class: A Baroque Comedy.*
Heinemann, London, UK, 1969.
Grove Press, New York, USA, 1969,
Paperback.
Methuen, London, UK, 1989,
Paperback.

A play which features the Ripper.

WILSON Colin   *The Killer.*
New English Library, London, UK,
1970, P/B.
Panther Books, London, UK, 1977,
Paperback.
Published in America as *"Lingard".*
Crown Books, New York, USA, 1970.
Pocket Books, New York, USA, 1972.

A story of a modern day Jack the Ripper.

SHEW Spencer   *Hands Of The Ripper.*
Sphere Books, London, UK, 1971, P/B.

A novelisation of the 1971 Hammer film starring Eric Porter and Angharad Rees.

GEORGE Theodore   *The Murders On The Square.*
Dodd & Mead, New York, USA, 1971.

A series of murders are committed to rival those of Jack the Ripper.

NEELY Richard   *The Walter Syndrome.*
                                   McCall Publishing, New York, USA,
                                   1970.
                                   Signet Books, New York, USA, 1971,
                                   Paperback (No. Y4766).

**A modern day Ripper known as 'The Executioner' strikes
fear into New York as he violates and mutilates women.**

HAYES R. Chetwynd   *The Unbidden.*
                                   Tandem Books, London, UK, 1971.

Includes the Ripper short story 'The Gatecrasher'.

BLISH James   *Star Trek 8.*
                                   Bantam Books, New York, USA, 1972,
                                   Paperback, Reprinted continually.
                                   Corgi Books, London, UK, 1973,
                                   Paperback, Reprinted 1984.

Includes Robert Bloch 'Wolf In The Fold'.

CASHMAN John   *The Gentleman From Chicago: Being An
                                   Account Of The Doings Of Neill Cream.*
                                   Harper & Row, New York, USA, 1973.
                                   Hamish Hamilton, London, UK, 1974.
                                   Popular Library, New York, USA, 1973,
                                   P/B.

**A fictional account of a possible Ripper suspect who was
actually in prison during the Whitechapel Murders.**

HUFF T.E.   *Nine Bucks Row.*
                                        Hawthorn Books, New York, USA,
                                        1973.
                                        Published in paperback under the title:
                                        'Susannah Beware'
                                        Dell Books, New York, USA, 1976,
                                        Paperback, (No. 6491). Reprinted
                                        September 1992, (different cover).

**Set in London 1888 a young woman believes she may be
falling in love with a man who may be responsible for the
Ripper murders. Recommended reading. The hardback
edition has a truly wonderful dustjacket. Both titles are
hard to find.**

RICE Jeff   *The Night Stalker.*
                                        Pocket Books, New York, USA, 1973,
                                        Paperback, Reprinted 1984.

SLADEK John   *Black Aura.*
                                        Jonathan Cape, London, UK, 1974.
                                        Panther Books, London, UK, 1975, P/B.

Puts forward Doctor Watson as a possible Ripper suspect.

ANON   *The Ballad of Jack the Ripper And Other
                             Cockney Songs - Volume 1.*
                                        Southern Music Publishing, England,
                                        1974.

Lists music and lyrics (23 pages).

GARDNER John   *The Return of Moriarty.*
                       Weidenfeld & Nicolson, London, UK,
                       1974.
                       Putnam, New York, USA, 1974.
                       Berkley Books, New York, USA, 1976,
                       Paperback, (No. T3095).
                       Berkley Books, New York, USA, 1981,
                       Reprinted, Paperback, (New Cover).
                       Issued in paperback in UK as:
                       'Moriarty'.
                       Pan Books, London, UK, 1976,
                       Paperback.
                       (A Book Club edition was issued by
                       Book Club Associates in hardback
                       around 1974).

MARAIS Marc   *Duel For A Dark Angel.*
                       New English Library, London, UK,
                       1975, P/B.

**A wave of sickening murders hit the streets of Paris. A
killer to rival that of Jack the Ripper is at large as the
bodies of mutilated women are discovered.**

BARRY John Brooks   *The Michaelmas Girls.*
                       Deutsch, London, UK, 1975.

**A highly recommended novel which sees the Ripper claim
six victims in Victorian London. We learn that the Ripper
was not working alone, but with a woman!
Barry spent time in Whitechapel studying the case in detail
before penning this excellent fictional account.**

PARRY Michel   *Jack The Knife: Tales of Jack the Ripper.*
                                             Mayflower Books, London, UK, 1975,
                                             P/B.

The first anthology of Ripper fiction. The book contains ten short stories based on Jack the Ripper.

PRONZINI Bill &   *The Running Of Beasts.*
MALZBERG Barry   Putnam, New York, USA, 1976.
                                             Fawcett Crest, New York, USA, 1979,
                                             P/B.

A homicidal maniac is on the loose as five women have been hideously murdered in the same style as the Ripper murders.

PEMBER Ron &   *Jack the Ripper: A Musical Play.*
DeMARNE Denis   Samuel French Ltd., London, UK,
                                             1976, P/B.
                                             Reprinted 1990's with a different cover
                                             (although still dated 1976!).

A play for eight men and eight women relating to the East End Murders. A solution to the Ripper's identity is hinted at (Druitt), but the play is an atmospheric commentary rather than an historical re-enactment.

HAMILL Edson T.   *The Slasher.*
                                             Leisure Books, New York, USA, 1976,
                                             Paperback, (No. 335 ZK).

A latter-day Jack the Ripper is back on the streets of New York murdering and mutilating prostitutes.

LOVESEY Peter   *Swing Swing Together.*
                                    MacMillan, London, UK, 1976.
                                    Dodd & Mead, New York, USA, 1976.
                                    Penguin Books, London, 1978,
                                    Paperback,
                                    Reprinted 1980, different cover.
                                    Arrow Books, London, UK, 1991, P/B.

           Chapter 14 "Touching on Jack the Ripper".

CHAPLIN Patrice   *By Flower And Dean Street: And The Love Apple.*
                                    Duckworth, London, UK, 1976.
                                    Methuen Books, London, UK, 1988,
                                    P/B.

           **Jack the Ripper makes a ghostly reappearance in modern
           day London when two people find themselves mysteriously
           possessed.**

ANDREWS Mark   *The Return Of Jack the Ripper.*
                                    Leisure Books, New York, USA, 1977,
                                    Paperback, (No. 476KK).

           **Just as an English acting company open on Broaodway
           with a play on the Jack the Ripper murders, a series of
           murders against prostitutes occur. A new Ripper, known
           as 'The Blade', was responsible.**

MORCAMBE
Eric &
WISE Ernest

The Morecambe And Wise Special.
Weidenfeld & Nicolson, London, UK,
1977.

Includes 'The Whitechapel Murders: A Tale of Sheerluck Holmes and Doctor Witsend'. Holmes and Watson seek JOCK the Ripper in this comedy spoof.

PARRY Michel
(Ed.)

Reign Of Terror: The Fourth Victorian Book Of Horror Stories.
Corgi Books, London, UK, 1978,
Paperback.

Contains two Ripper short stories including Hume Nisbet - 'The Demon Spell'.

PARRY Michel
(Ed.)

Christopher Lee's Omnibus Of Evil.
W.H. Allen, London, UK, 1978.
Granada, London, UK, 1980,
Paperback.

Includes Theodora Benson – "Jack the Ripper" Ray Russell - "Sagitarius".

McKAY Kenneth

Shadow Of The Knife.
Playboy Press, New York, USA, 1978,
Paperback. Reprinted 1982, Paperback
(No.Z1048)

A modern Ripper, known as the Nassau Slasher, who mutilates his women victims.

NEWTON Mike   *The Hunter No. 1: The Ripper.*
                                  Publisher's Consultants, California,
                                  USA, 1978,
                                  Paperback, (No. HUN 3001).

A novel which sees random sadistic slayings of prostitutes in Los Angeles committed by a killer known as The Ripper.

HALL John   *Jack The Ripper Poems.*
                                  Greenhouse Review Press, Santa Cruz,
                                  USA, 1978.

A book which contains seven poems on the Ripper which is very hard to locate due to a small print run. Only 350 copies were produced with the first 50 signed and numbered by the author.

DIBDIN Michael   *The Last Sherlock Holmes Story.*
                                  Jonathan Cape, London, UK, 1978.
                                  Pantheon Books, New York, USA,
                                  1978.
                                  Ballantine Books, New York, USA,
                                  1979,
                                  Paperback, (No. 28067).
                                  Vintage Books, New York, USA, 1996,
                                  P/B.
                                  Sphere Books, London, UK, 1980,
                                  Paperback.
                                  Faber & Faber, London, UK, 1989,
                                  Paperback,
                                  Reprinted with corrections, 1990,
                                  Paperback.
                                  Oxford University Press, Oxford, UK,
                                  1995,
                                  Reprinted 1996 and 1997, Paperbacks.

A novel which sees the World's greatest detective, Sherlock Holmes, tackle the World's greatest criminal Jack the Ripper.

ST. MARTIN   *Jill.*
Thomas   Dell Books, New York, USA, 1979,
                                Paperback,
                                (No. 14230).

**A female version of Jack the Ripper stalks the streets and
revels in blood - and no man is safe from her.**

STEVENS Shane   *By Reason Of Insanity.*
                                Simon & Schuster, New York, USA,
                                1979.
                                Weidenfeld & Nicolson, London, UK,
                                1979.

A man pursues a Ripper type career in America.

BYRON COVER   *An East Wind Coming.*
Arthur   Berkley Books, New York, USA, 1979,
                                P/B.

**An immortal Sherlock Holmes faces a deathless Jack the
Ripper in a fantasy duel through the corridors of time.**

WEVERKA Robert   *Murder By Decree.*
                                Ballantine Books, New York, USA,
                                1979,
                                Paperback, (No. 28062).
                                Corgi Books, London, UK, 1980,
                                Paperback.

**This is the novelisation of the 1979 film of the same name
starring Christopher Plummer and James Mason.   The
American edition, by Ballantine, is illustrated with stills
taken from the film. The UK edition has no illustrations.**

ALEXANDER Karl   *Time After Time.*

> Delacorte Press, New York, USA, 1979.
> Dell Books, New York, USA, 1979,
> Paperback, (No. 18804).
> Granada Publishing, London, UK,
> 1980, P/B.

The novelisation of the 1979 Warner Bros. film starring Malcolm McDowell and David Warner. H.G. Wells chases Jack the Ripper in a time machine to 1979 San Francisco to try to rid the world of the infamous killer.

GORDON Richard   *The Private Life Of Jack The Ripper.*

> Heinemann, London, UK, 1980.
> Published in America as -
> *Jack the Ripper.*
> Atheneum, New York, USA, 1980.

A novel set in 1888 has a doctor responsible for the Ripper killings.

SILVERSTONE Lou   *The Mad Book Of Mysteries.*
(Mad Magazine)

> Warner Books, New York, USA, 1980,
> P/B.

Includes 'The Return Of The Ripper' featuring Shamus Holmes and Doctor Whatso in this book of detective pastiches. Illustrated by Jack Rickard.

COSGROVE-   *Bride Of Fury.*
PAYES Rachael

> Playboy Press, New York, USA, 1980,
> Paperback, (No. 16592).

The book written for 'Jack The Bodice-Ripper' sees a woman (Kate Kingsley) wonder if her husband is responsible for the Whitechapel killings which are taking place.

BAGLEY Desmond   *Crime Wave.*
                                    William Collins, London, UK, 1981.

Includes the short story 'The Case Of The Baker Street Dozen' by Arthur Douglas.

DOBSON William   *The Ripper.*
                                    Signet Books, New York, USA, 1981,
                                    Paperback, (No. 451).

A modern day Jack the Ripper stalks the streets of 1982 London, killing and butchering young women.

DUDLEY William E.   *The Untold Sherlock Holmes.*
                                    Hansom Press, New York, USA, 1982.

Chapter 3 entitled 'Jack the Ripper'.

PAUL Raymond   *The Thomas Street Horror.*
                                    Viking Press, New York, USA, 1982.

LIEBOW Ely M.   *Doctor Joe Bell: Model For Sherlock Holmes.*
                                    Bowling Green University Press, Ohio,
                                    USA, 1982.

Includes 'Jack the Ripper'.

TINE Robert   *Uneasy Lies The Head.*
                                    Viking Press, New York, USA, 1982.
                                    Collins Crime Club, London, UK, 1983.
                                    Pinnacle Books, New York, USA, 1985,
                                    P/B.

A modern version of Jack the Ripper is stalking London's streets.

KURLAND Michael   *Death By Gaslight.*
                                    Signet Books, New York, USA, 1982,
                                    Paperback, (No. 451).

**A killer who made Jack the Ripper seem gentle was slitting
the throats of England's aristocracy.**

PINCHER Chapman   *The Private World Of St. John Terrapin.*
                                    Sidgwick & Jackson, London, UK,
                                    1982.

MACDONALD   *Tessa D'Arblay*
Malcolm Ross
                                    St. Martins Press, New York, USA,
                                    1983.
                                    Hodder & Stoughton, London, UK,
                                    1983.
                                    Book Club Associates, London, UK,
                                    1983.

**The novel surrounds a young woman living in Victorian
London in 1888 and features Dr. Jekyll, Dracula and Jack
the Ripper.**

ELLISON Harlan   *Partners In Wonder.*
                                    Ace Books, New York, USA, 1983,
                                    Paperback.

Contains two Jack the Ripper short stories:
  i). Robert Bloch – A Toy For Juliette.
  **ii). Harlan Ellison – The Prowler In The City At The
  Edge Of The World.**

FARMER Philip Jose   *Gods Of The Riverworld.*
                                    Putnam, New York, USA, 1983.
                                    Panther Books, London, UK, 1984,
                                    Paperback.

NO AUTHOR

Murder Most Foul.
Octopus Books, London, 1984,
Paperback.

Anthology which includes: Thomas Burke - 'The Hands of Mr. Ottermole'.

HOCH Edward D.

The Quests Of Simon Ark.
Mysterious Press, New York, USA,
1984.

Contains 'The Treasure Of Jack the Ripper'.

WALSH Ray

The Mycroft Memoranda.
St. Martin's Press, New York, USA,
1984.
Deutsch, London, UK, 1984.

Drawing on Doctor Watson's diary and Sherlock Holmes' own notebook the author reveals that Holmes did track down and identify the Ripper.

BLOCH Robert

The Night Of The Ripper.
Doubleday & Co., New York, USA,
1984.
Tor Books, New York, USA, 1986,
Paperback.
Robert Hale, London, UK, 1986.
Grafton Books, London, UK, 1986,
Paperback,
Reprinted 1987.

An excellent novel which sees a young American doctor, as well as Detective Abberline, realise that all the Ripper murders have taken place near the London hospital. Could a surgeon be responsible for the crimes?

GARDEN Graeme   *I'm Sorry I'll Read That Again: The*
& ODDIE Bill   *Classic Scripts.*

                                        Javelin Books, London, UK, 1985,
                                        Paperback.

               Includes 'Jack the Ripper' - a comedy sketch.

FARMER   *Dayworld.*
Philip Jose
                                        Granada Books, London, UK, 1985,
                                        Paperback.

PRONZINI Bill &   *The Giant Book Of Horror Stories.*
MALZBERG Barry &   Castle Books, New Jersey, USA
GREENBERG Martin   1985.
(Eds.)   Magpie Books, London, 1991,
                                        Paperback.

               Includes Robert Bloch - 'Yours Truly - Jack the Ripper'.

TROW M.J.   *The Adventures Of Inspector Lestrade.*
                                        MacMillan, London, UK, 1985.
                                        Published in America as;
                                        The Supreme Adventures of Inspector
                                        Lestrade.
                                        Stein & Day, New York, USA, 1985.

ETCHISON Dennis   *Cutting Edge.*
                                        Doubleday & Co., New York, USA,
                                        1986.
                                        Futura, London, UK, 1987, Paperback.
                                        Includes William F. Nolan - 'The Final
                                        Stone'.

SHANNON Dell   *Chaos Of Crime.*
William Morrow, New York, USA,
1985.
Gollancz, London, UK, 1986.
Worldwide Books, New York, USA,
1989, Paperback, (No. 26015).

Luis Mendoza and the Los Angeles police face a modern version of Jack the Ripper amongst their cases.

BOROWITZ Albert   *The Jack the Ripper Walking Tour Murder.*
St. Martin's Press, New York, USA,
1986.

A member of a Jack the Ripper walking tour is murdered. Or was it an accident?

HARPER Leslie   *The Secret Conan Doyle Correspondence.*
Hascomb Press, Utah, USA, 1986,
Paperback.

The story concerns a Ripper type murder in New York.

THOMAS Donald *The Ripper's Apprentice.*
St. Martin's Press, New York, USA,
1986.
MacMillan, London, UK, 1986.
Papermac, London, UK, 1988,
Paperback.

A fictionalisation of the real crimes of Neill Cream who was also a Ripper suspect.

WEST Pamela

Yours Truly Jack the Ripper.

St. Martin's Press, New York, USA, 1987.
Dell Books, New York, USA, 1989, Paperback.

Set in London in 1888, Inspector West tries to track down Jack the Ripper and discovers an official cover up; well engineered and very shocking.

LINDSAY Fredric

Jill Rips.

Deutsch, London, UK, 1987.
Corgi Books, London, UK, 1988, Paperback.

A series of murders are committed in Glasgow very similar to those which occurred one hundred years earlier in London's East End. Only this time it is not Jack the Ripper but JILL the Ripper.

SINCLAIR Iain

Whitechapell Scarlet Tracings.

Goldmark, Rutland, UK, 1987.
Paladin Books, London, UK, 1988, Paperback.
Vintage Books, London, UK, 1995, Paperback.
Granta Books, London, UK, 1998, Paperback.

An excellent novel where a group of antiquarian book-sellers conduct an investigation into the Ripper murders.

CLARK Mark   *Ripper.*
> Byren House, Ontario, Canada, 1987.
> Berkley Books, New York, USA, 1989,
> Paperback.

Set during the Ripper murders this novel takes the reader eventually to the streets of Whitechapel on the trail of Jack the Ripper. Recommended.

LORE SMITH   *Yours Truly Jack the Ripper.*
Terence
> St. Martin's Press, New York, USA,
> 1987.
> St. Martin's Press, New York, USA,
> 1988, P/B.
> Grafton Books, London, UK, 1988,
> Paperback.

One hundred years later Jack the Ripper is back, reliving his crimes, corpse by bloody corpse.

PRONZINI Bill &   *Suspicious Characters.*
GREENBERG Martin
> Ivy Books, New York, USA, 1987.

Includes Edward D. Hoch - 'The Treasure of Jack The Ripper'.

DE NOUX O'Neil   *Grim Reaper.*
> Zebra Books, New York, USA, 1988,
> Paperback, reprinted 1991.

Terror prowls the Louisiana night, a killer of women known to the media as 'The Slasher', but only the madman knows his identity - Jack of the Night: Jack the Ripper.

HAWKE Simon   *The Wizard Of Whitechapel.*
                                        Popular Library, New York, USA, 1988,
                                        P/B.

**A wizard called Wyrdrune travels back to 1888 London
and attempts to stop Jack the Ripper carrying out his
murders.**

SCOTT Chris   *Jack.*
                                        MacMillan, Ontario, Canada, 1988.
                                        Seal Books, Toronto, Canada, 1989,
                                        Paperback.

**The author attempts to prove Doctor Neill Cream was
indeed Jack the Ripper in this novel which is well worth
tracking down.**

DANIEL Mark   *Jack the Ripper.*
                                        Penguin Books, London, UK, 1988,
                                        Paperback.
                                        Signet Books, New York, USA, 1988,
                                        Paperback.

**Based on the Thames television series - Jack the Ripper
starring Michael Caine and Lewis Collins shown in 1988.**

TROW M.J.   *Lestrade And The Ripper.*
                                        MacMillan, London, UK, 1988.

**A novel also featuring Sherlock Holmes and Doctor Watson
where the Ripper murders, as well as another series of
murders, apparently unrelated, test Inspector Lestrade.**

CASPER Susan & DOZOIS Gardner	*Jack the Ripper.*
	Futura Books, London, UK, 1988, Pa perback.
	Published in America as *'Ripper'.*
	Tor Books, New York, USA, 1988, Paperback.

An anthology of Ripper fiction containing nineteen short stories.

GREENBERG Martin & WAUGH Charles & McSHERRY Frank (Eds)	*Red Jack.*
	Daw Books, New York, USA, 1988, Paperback, (No. 766).

An anthology of Ripper fiction containing eight short stories plus an introduction.

GELB Jeff & FRIEND Lonn	*Hot Blood: Tales Of Provocative Murder.*
	Pocket Books, New York, USA, 1989.

Includes two Ripper short stories -
i) **Chet Williamson - Blood Night.**
ii) **David J. Schow - Red Light.**

IRVINE Robert	*The Angels' Share.*
	St. Martin's Press, New York, USA, 1989.
	Pocket Books, New York, USA, 1990, Paperback.

A modern day Jack the Ripper out to bring down the Latter Day Saints in Salt Lake City.

TRENCH Jason   *The Hammer.*

> Doubleday Crime Club Books, New York, USA,1989.

A series of murders committed by a modern day Jack the Ripper.

READER Barbara   *Jack the Ripper Part II*

> Excalibur Press, London, UK, 1989, Paperback.

A spate of Ripper style murders occur and the hunt for the elusive Jack the Ripper II is underway.

SUTCLIFFE   *Loves Illusion.*
Katherine

> Onyx Books, New York, USA 1989.
> Topaz Books, New York, USA, 1998, Paperback, (No. JE 836).

A romance novel heavily featuring Jack the Ripper.

ARCHER Rodney &   *The Harlots Curse.*
JONES Powell

> Preston Editions, London, UK, 1990, P/B.

This play tells of the life of Mary Kelly, the Ripper's final victim. It was first performed in 1986 at the Old Synagogue Theatre in London.

GEORGE Stephen R.   *Grandma's Little Darling.*

> Zebra Books, New York, USA, 1990, P/B.

MAXIM John R.   *The Bannerman Effect.*

> Bantam Books, New York, USA, 1990, P/B.

ELLIS Wesley *Lone Star And The Ripper.*
Jove Books, New York, USA, 1990,
Paperback, (No. 93).

A series of murders occur in St. Louis similar to those of Jack the Ripper and it's up to the heroes Jessie and Ki to capture this mad slasher.

BIDERMAN Bob *Judgement Of Death.*
Gollancz, London, UK, 1989.
Gollancz Crime, London, UK,
1990, Paperback.

An investigative journalist in London compares two sensational poison trials in this novel which also features a frightened doctor, multi-millionaire and Jack the Ripper.

McCARTY John *Deadly Resurrection.*
St. Martin's Press, New York,
USA, 1990, P/B.

Brutal death stalks the streets of Holbrook. More viciously depraved than even London's Jack the Ripper, the Holbrook Ripper leaves behind no clues.

WEST Paul *The Women Of Whitechapel.*
Serpents Tail, London, UK, 1991.
Published in America as
The Women Of Whitechapel And Jack the Ripper.
Random House, New York, USA,
1991.
Overlook Press, New York, USA,
1992, P/B.

A most enjoyable novel based around Stephen Knight's theory. It is through the eyes of Walter Sickert that we discover why the prostitutes were murdered and by whom.

LEVINE Paul	*Night Vision.*
	Bantam, New York, USA, 1991,
	Paperback.

Detective Jack Lassiter tracks down a modern day version of Jack the Ripper.

SATTERHWAIT	*Wilde West.*
Walter	St. Martin's Press, New York,
	USA, 1991.

A series of prostitutes are murdered far out west in this novel which also features Oscar Wilde.

SHANNON Dell	*Destiny Of Death.*
	Worldwide, New York, USA,
	1991, Paperback.

A novel which features Jack the Stripper.

McCOY Edmund	*Blood Of The Fathers.*
	Orion Books, London, UK, 1992.
	Orion Books, London, UK, 1993,
	Paperback.

An executive publisher discovers some disturbing facts about his father in this novel which features Jack the Ripper and the I.R.A.

HANNA Edward B.	*The Whitechapel Horrors: A Sherlock Holmes Novel.*
	Carroll & Graf, New York, USA,
	1992.
	Carroll & Graf, New York, USA,
	1993, P/B.

Sherlock Holmes is called in to catch and unmask Jack the Ripper.

BAILEY Hilary   *The Cry From Street To Street.*
                                    Constable, London, UK, 1992, Re
                                    printed 1993.
                                    Constable, London, UK, 1992. Large
                                    Paperback edition.
                                    Pan Books, London, UK, 1993, Paper
                                    back,
                                    (different cover).

                      **The story of the Ripper's last victim Mary Kelly and her
                      life in Victorian London during Jack the Ripper's reign.**

McCRUMB Sharyn   *Missing Susan.*
                                    Random House, New York, USA, 1991.
                                    Ballantine Books, New York, USA,
                                    1992,
                                    Paperback, (No. 37945) Reprinted 1992
                                    with a different cover.

                      **A novel set during a Jack the Ripper walking tour in
                      London which cunningly features versions of Martin Fido
                      (Rowan Rover), Paul Begg (Kenneth O'Connor) and
                      Donald Rumbelow.**

WALLACE Randall   *Where Angels Watch.*
                                    Bantam, New York, USA, 1992,
                                    Paperback.

                      Jack the Ripper returns to Los Angeles.

AYCLIFFE Jonathan   *Naomi's Room.*
                                    Harper Collins, London & New York,
                                    1992.

                      **The phantom of Jack the Ripper returns to Cambridge,
                      England.**

NEWMAN Kim   *Anno Dracula.*
                                    Simon & Schuster, London, UK, 1992.
                                    Carroll & Graf, New York, USA, 1993.
                                    Pocket Books, London, UK, 1993,
                                    Paperback.
                                    Avon Books, New York, USA, 1994,
                                    P/B.

An excellent novel set in London in 1888 and featuring Queen Victoria, Count Dracula and, of course, Jack the Ripper.

McGUIRE Christine   *Until Proven Guilty.*
                                    Pocket Books, New York, USA, 1993,
                                    P/B.

A story of a modern day Jack the Ripper killing prostitutes.

O'NEILL Gilda   *Whitechapel Girl.*
                                    Headline, London, UK, 1993.
                                    Headline, London, UK, 1994,
                                    Paperback.

A novel set in London's East End during the reign of Jack the Ripper.

PENSWICK Neil   *The New Doctor Who Adventures: The Pit.*
                                    Doctor Who Books, Virgin Publishing,
                                    London, UK, 1993, Paperback.

A Doctor Who adventure featuring the Whitechapel Murders.

LAYMON Richard   *Savage.*

> Headline, London, UK, 1993.
> Headline, London, UK, 1993,
> Paperback.
> St. Martin's Press, New York, USA,
> 1994.

A fifteen year old boy witnesses Jack the Ripper murder Mary Kelly and years later he brings the horrors of the Ripper to New York.

FROST Mark   *The List Of Seven.*

> Hutchinson, London, UK, 1993.
> Arrow Books, London, UK, 1994,
> Paperback.

Includes the creator of Sherlock Holmes, Sir Arthur Conan Doyle as a Ripper suspect.

ZELAZNY Roger   *A Night In The Lonesome October.*

> Avo Nova Morrow, New York, USA,
> 1993
> Avo Nova, New York, USA, 1994,
> Paperback.
> Orbit Books, London, UK, 1994,
> Paperback.

In the London gloom, Jack the Ripper prowls the streets with his faithful watchdog, Snuff.

ODOM Mel   *Stalker Analog.*

> Roc, New York, USA, 1993, Paperback.

A Ripper is on the loose and is trailed by a female cop in this futuristic thriller.

STUART Anne   *Break The Night.*
                      Silhouette Books, Shadow Book 9, New
                      York,
                      USA, 1993, Paperback.
                      Silhouette Books, Surrey, UK, 1996,
                      Paperback,
                      (No. 108).

                      **A modern day version of Jack the Ripper strikes in Los
                      Angeles.**

SANDFORD John   *Night Prey.*
                      Putnam, New York, USA, 1994.

                      Jack the Ripper in Minneapolis.

BUFALINO   *The Keeper Of Ruins And Other Inventions.*
Gesualdo   Harvill, London, UK, 1994.

                      **Includes the short story - London Nightpiece. Originally
                      published as *L'Uomo Invaso* in Italy in 1986.**

POLLOCK Sharon   *Saucy Jack.*
                      Blizzard Publishing, Winnipeg, Canada,
                      1994, P/B.

                      **A play on Jack the Ripper featuring only four characters,
                      J.K. Stephen, Montague Druitt, Prince Eddy and Kate, a
                      music hall entertainer. It was first produced by the Garry
                      Theatre, Calgary, Canada on 25th November 1993.**

ACKROYD Peter   *Dan Leno And The Limehouse Golem.*
                                          Sinclair Stevenson, London, UK, 1994.
                                          Minerva, London, UK, 1995,
                                          Paperback.

                        Not a Ripper novel as such, but still a story of multiple murder set only a few years before the Whitechapel murders.

MITCHELSON   *The Baker Street Irregular.*
Austin   Ian Henry Publications, Essex, UK,
                                          1994.

                        This unauthorised biography of Sherlock Holmes includes 'The Curious Incident of Sherlock Holmes and the Whitechapel Murders'.

BAILEY Hilary   *The Strange Adventures Of Charlotte Holmes:*
                        Sister Of The More Famous Sherlock.
                                          Constable, London, UK, 1994.

                        Includes a chapter 'An Adventure In Whitechapel'.

SLADE Michael   *Ripper.*
                                          Hodder & Stoughton, London, UK,
                                          1994.
                                          Hodder & Stoughton, London, UK,
                                          1995, P/B.
                                          Black River, New York, USA, 1994.
                                          Signet Books, New York, USA, 1994,
                                          P/B.

                        Jack the Ripper returns and strikes fear into America - murdering America's foremost feminist.

| MOORE Alan | *From Hell: The Complete Scripts.* |
| | Borderlands Press, Brooklandville, USA, 1994, Paperback. |

The scripts of the 'From Hell' graphic novel series in book form.

| DICKINSON Joe | *Jack The Ripper - Monster Of Whitechapel.* |
| | Bakers Plays, Boston, USA, 1995, . |

A play on Jack the Ripper which was first performed on 28th March 1986 at the Pocket Sandwich Theatre, Dallas in Texas. Features Annie Chapman, Kate Eddowes, Sir Charles Warren and Forbes Winslow.

| ROBERTS J.R. | *The Gunsmith (No. 165): The Denver Ripper.* |
| | Jove Books, New York, USA, 1995, Paperback. |

A Ripper is on the loose in this all action Western novel.

HAINING Peter	*Tales From The Rogues Gallery.*
	Little & Brown, London, UK, 1994.
	Warner Books, London, UK, 1995, Paperback.

An anthology of fiction which includes two Ripper short stories:
i) Anthony Boucher - A Kind Of Madness.
ii) Ramsey Campbell - Jack's Little Friend.

| JOHNSON Dennis | *Ripper: The Official Strategy Guide.* |
| | Prima Publishing, USA, 1996, Paperback. |

Not a novel, but a guide to the computer game. Only a true completist should track this title down.

PERRY Anne   *Pentecost Alley.*
                              Fawcett, New York, USA, 1996.
                              Fawcett, New York, USA, 1997, P/B.

After sending a man to the gallows for the murder of a Whitechapel prostitute two years after Jack the Ripper's reign of terror, Thomas Pitt is confronted with another similar killing that causes speculation that the wrong man has been hanged for being the Ripper and that the real Jack may have returned.

SOMTOW S.P.   *Vanitas.*
                              Tor Books, New York, USA, 1996,
                              Paperback.

WALKER Fred   *I Love My Work.*
                              Questex, Ontario, Canada, 1996,
                              Paperback.

Subtitle: - A Ripping Good Play. A most enjoyable play featuring Sherlock Holmes and Jack the Ripper. Characters include Caroline Maxwell, Mary Kelly and Inspector Lestrade.

STAPLES   *The Ghost Of Whitechapel.*
Mary Jane   Corgi Books, London, UK, 1997,
                              Paperback.

The spectre of Jack the Ripper returns to haunt London's East End in 1900.

RUSSELL Jay   *Burning Bright.*
                              Raven Books, London, UK, 1997,
                              Paperback.

A novel with a rather obscure Ripper link.

THOR Raymond   *Bloodguilty.*
                               Danger Publishing, California, USA,
                               1997.

                     **A novel which features Sherlock Holmes and Jack the
                     Ripper in which a 100 year old diary identifies the Ripper.**

RAINER Claire   *Fifth Member.*
                               Michael Joseph, London, UK, 1997.

                     **A series of murders take place which follow the same
                     pattern as those of Jack the Ripper. Time is running out
                     as Superintendent Gus Barnabus knows only five
                     murders will be committed.**

EDWARDS Martin   *Eve Of Destruction.*
                               Judy Piatkus, London, UK, 1996.
                               Judy Piatkus, London, UK, 1997,
                               Paperback.

                     **Not exactly a Ripper novel but one which features James
                     Maybrick and Battlecrease House.**

SUSTER Gerald   *The Labyrinth Of Satan.*
                               Hodder & Stoughton, London, UK,
                               1997.

                     **It's 1894 and the adventurer Sir Percy Sulgrave is sure
                     that Jack the Ripper is still alive and stalking the streets.**

HOLLAND Tom   *Supping With Panthers.*
                              Little & Brown, London, UK, 1996.
                              Warner Books, London, UK, 1997,
                              Paperback.
                              Published in America as:
                              Slave Of My Thirst.
                              Pocket Books, New York, USA, 1996.

A novel featuring Vampires, Oscar Wilde, Bram Stoker, Lord Byron and Jack the Ripper in the gaslit streets of Victorian London.

HARPER Andrew   *Bad Karma.*
                              Kensington, New York, USA, 1997.

A modern day tale featuring a woman who thinks she was the girlfriend of Jack the Ripper in a previous life. Contains flashbacks to Whitechapel 1888 featuring the Ripper.

SOARES Jo   *A Samba For Sherlock.*
                              Pantheon, New York, USA, 1997.
                              Vintage Books, New York, 1998,
                              Paperback.

A serial killer of women in South America is being tracked by Sherlock Holmes. The killer leaves for London in 1888 and decides to become Jack the Ripper.

BLOCH Robert   *Robert Bloch's Psychos.*
(Ed.)   Pocket Books, London, UK, 1997,
                              Paperback.

Includes Denise M. Bruchman- 'The Lesser Of Two Evils'

HARWARD Janet   *Echoes Of Death.*

                                    O'Neill Publishing, Birmingham, UK,
                                    1998, P/B.

                       **A series of murders occur in Torquay and Detective
                       Inspector Josephine Blake is convinced that the killer is
                       deliberately imitating Jack the Ripper.**

PERRY Robert &   *Doctor Who: Matrix.*
TUCKER Mike
                                    BBC Worldwide, London, UK, 1998,
                                    Paperback.

                       **Doctor Who's time machine, the Tardis, is drawn to London
                       in the winter of 1888 where he meets Jack the Ripper.**

ROBERTS Barry   *Sherlock Holmes And The Royal Flush.*
                                    Constable, London, UK, 1998.

                       **A novel set in 1887 which sees Ripper suspect Dr. Francis
                       Tumblety battle with Sherlock Holmes. At the end of the
                       book there is a two page discussion on whether Tumblety
                       could have been Jack the Ripper.**

HARRIS Don R.   *Foggy Night Murders.*

                                    Four Seasons Publishers, Florida, USA,
                                    1998, P/B.

                       **An upper class medical student is forced to become a
                       gambler, sailor and gold prospector. Accused by Scotland
                       Yard of being Jack the Ripper, he must discover the truth.
                       Is he a killer or a victim?**

ANSELL Derek   *The Whitechapel Murders.*
                                    Citron Press, London, UK, 1999,
                                    Paperback

                       A 'factional' account of the Ripper murders, revealed from
                       the letters, diaries and journals of James and Florence
                       Maybrick.

BUCHANAN   *Ripper.*
Carl Jay   University of South Carolina Press,
                                    USA, 1999,
                                    Hardback and Paperback.

                       Edited by Richard Howard and released as part of the
                       James Dickey contemporary poetry series. This is a book
                       of poems all relating to the Jack the Ripper case featuring
                       both victims and suspects.

PAUL Barbara   *Jack Be Quick And Other Crime Stories.*
                                    Five Star Standard Print Mystery Series,
                                    USA, 1999.

                       Contains thirty short stories, the first one being "Jack Be
                       Quick" which features the Ripper and is set in Whitechapel
                       in 1888.

Foreign Language Translations Of Ripper Fiction.

BELLOC
LOWNDES
Mrs. Marie

Den Logerende.

Denmark, 1923, Reprinted 1958.

Danish edition of 'The Lodger'.

BELLOC
LOWNDES
Mrs. Marie

De Wreker.

Hollandsche Biblioteek, Haarlem,
Netherlands.
Not dated, circa 1930's.

Dutch edition of 'The Lodger'.

ALEXANDER David

Terreur A Broadway.

Gallimard, France, 1955, Serie Noire,
No. 225.

French edition of Terror on Broadway.

WILSON Colin

Der Schacht Zu Babel.

Wien, Stuttgart, Germany, 1961.

German edition of 'Ritual In The Dark'.

WILSON Colin

Ritual I Moruet.

Denmark, 1962.

Danish edition of "Ritual In The Dark'.

BROWN Fredric

Der Ripper Van Chicago.

Pabel, Baden, Germany, 1965.

German edition of 'The Screaming Mimi'.

QUEEN Ellery   *Sherlock Holmes Contre Jack L'Eventreur.*
                                      Editions Stock, Paris, France, 1968.
                                        Editions Jai Lu, Paris, France, 1989.

French edition of 'Sherlock Holmes versus Jack the Ripper'.

QUEEN Ellery   *Et Studie I Mord.*
                                        Denmark, 1968.

Danish edition of 'A Study In Terror'.

QUEEN Ellery   *Sherlock Holmes Gegen Jack The Ripper.*
                                      Ullstein Buch, Frankfurt, Germany, 1968.
                                      Reprinted as 'Sherlock Holmes Und Jack The Ripper Eine Studie Des Schrechens.
                                      Du Mont, Koln, Germany, 1989, reprinted 1993.

German editions of 'A Study In Terror'.

BLOCH Robert   *Jack The Ripper: Der Mantel.*
                                        Luther, Baden-Baden, Germany, 1971.
                                        German edition of 'Yours Truly Jack The Ripper'.

BELLOC   *Jack The Ripper Oder Er Untermieter.*
LOWNDES   Diogenes, Germany, 1974, Reprinted 1983.

German edition of 'The Lodger'.

HUFF T.E.   *L'Assassin Rode Dans L'Impasse.*
                                        Presses De La Cite, Paris, France,
                                        1975.

                        French edition of 'Nine Bucks Row'.

GARDNER John   *Le Retour De Moriarty.*
                                        Edition Lattes, Paris France, 1976.
                                        Edition Oswald, France, 1984.

                        French edition of 'The Return Of Moriarty'.

SHEW Spencer   *Die Morderhande.*
                                        Pabel, Baden, Germany, 1976.

                        German edition of 'Hands Of The Ripper'.

BARNES Peter   *The Ruling Class: A Baroque Comedy.*
                                        Diesterweg. Munich, Germany, 1976.

ALEXANDER Karl   *Vluchten In Detijd.*
                                        De Kern, Bussum, Netherlands, 1979.

                        Dutch edition of 'Time After Time'.

St. MARTIN   *La Coupeuse De Tet Es.*
Thomas   Gallimard, Paris, France, 1980.

                        French edition of 'Jill'.

PRONZINI Bill &   *Jagt Die Bestie.*
MALZBERG Barry   Goldmann, Munich, Germany, 1981.

                        German edition of 'The Running Of Beasts'.

| BELLOC LOWNDES Mrs. Marie | *Was De Huurder Jack The Ripper.* |
| | Loeb, Amsterdam, Netherlands, 1981. |

Dutch edition of 'The Lodger'.

| DIBDIN Michael | *Der Letzte Sherlock Holmes Roman.* |
| | Goldmann, Munich, Germany, 1980. |

German edition of 'The Last Sherlock Holmes Story'.

| ALEXANDER Karl | *Flucht Ins Heute.* |
| | Heyne Bucher, Munich, Germany, 1983. |

German edition of 'Time After Time'.

| BLOCH Robert | *L'Eventreur.* |
| | Pocket, Fleuve Noir, Paris, France, 1983. |

French edition of 'The Will To Kill'.

| BLOCH Robert | *Aangenaam, Jack The Ripper.* |
| | Loeb, Amsterdam, Netherlands, 1985. |

Dutch edition of 'Yours Truly Jack The Ripper'.

| BLOCH Robert | *Der Ripper.* |
| | Heyne Bucher, Munich, Germany, 1987. |

German edition of 'The Night Of The Ripper'.

BLOCH Robert   *La Nuit De L'Eventreur.*
                                  Editions Clancier-Guenaud, Paris,
                                  France, 1988.

French edition of 'The Night Of The Ripper'.

DOBSON William   *L'Eventreur.*
                                  Fleuve Noir, Paris, France, 1989.
                                  Gore series No. 86.

French edition of 'The Ripper'.

WEST Paul   *The Women Of Whitechapel.*
                                  Editions Rivage, Papris, France, 1991.

DIBDIN Michael   *L'Ultime Defi De Sherlock Holmes.*
                                  Editions Payot et Rivages, France,
                                  1994.

French edition of 'The Last Sherlock Holmes Story'.

TROW M.J.   *Lestrade Und Jack The Ripper.*
                                  Rowohlt, Hamburg, Germany, 1994.

German edition of 'Lestrade And The Ripper'.

BLOCH Robert   *Jack Lo Squartatore.*
                                  RCS Libri & Grandi Opere, Milan, Italy,
                                  1994.

Italian edition of 'The Night Of The Ripper'.

NEWMAN Kim   *Anno Dracula.*
                                  Haffmans Verlag, Leipzig, Germany,
                                  1994.

German edition of 'Anno Dracula'.

The following fictional works are all Ripper related and have, so far, not been published in the English language. They are still worth tracking down even if it is only for the decorative and Ripperish covers the possess.

PAUL Adolf   *Uppskararen.*
                              Utgivningsar, Finland, 1892.

                   A 160 page novel which translates as 'The Ripper'.

VERHULST Raf   *Jack The Ripper.*
                            Belgium 1894.

ANON   *Huru Jack Uppskararen Blev Tillfangaten.*
                            Stockholm, Sweden, 1901.

                   No. 18 in a series called 'Sherlock Holmes Detective Stories'. The title translates as 'How Jack The Ripper Was Caught'.

ANON   *Les Dossiers Secrets Du Roi Des Detectives -*
           Jack L'Eventreur.
                            Fernand Laven, France, February 1908.
                            No. 16 in the series.
                            Reprinted from Germany where it was
                            originally published as:
                            Aus Den Geheimakten Des Welt
                            Detektivs.
                            Germany 1907 (No. 18 in series).
                            Reprinted in Hungary as: *Jack A*
                            Hasfelmetso - Szemelvenyek Egy
                            Sherlock Holmes Vilag - Detektiv Titkos
                            Aktailbol. Hungary, 1908, (No. 1 in
                            series).
                            Reprinted in Portugal as: *Dossiers*
                            Secrets Du Roi Des Detectives - Jack
                            O'Estripador. Portugal, 1909,
                            (No. 19 in series).

ANRI Pol

Jack The Ripper: Of Eene Misgreep Blijspel In Een Bedrif.

Janseens, Antwerp, Belgium, 1910, (No. 242).

ANON

Memorias Intimas De Sherlock Holmes: Jack El Destripador.

Edition Atlante, Barcelona, Spain, 1912.

DESNOS Robert

La Liberte Ou L'Amour Suivi De Deuil.

Editions Gallimard, France, 1927.
Reprinted as 'Jack L'Eventreur".
Editions Allia, Paris, France, 1997.

DUBNOPAC A.R.

Jack L'Eventreur.

France, no date, circa 1920's.

MAC ORLAN Pierre

La Tradition De Miniut.

Editions Emile Paul Freres, Paris, France, 1930.

GALOPIN Arnould

L'Homme Au Complet Gris.

Editions Albin Michel, Paris, France, 1931.

DE LORDE Andre & CHAINE Pierre & BAUCHE Henri

Grand Guignol: Jack L'Eventreur, L'Horrible Passion - Magie Noire.

Editions Eugene Figuiere, Paris, France, 1936.

A play in three acts with eighty four pages on the Ripper. The play was produced on 30th September 1934 at the Grand Guignol Theatre in Paris. It was adapted for French radio as 'Jack L'Eventreur' by Pierre Chaine and broadcast on 12th November 1986. The script was fifty one pages long.

125

BORDEWIJK Ferdinand	*Vijf Fantastische Vertellingen.* Nijgh & Van Ditmar, Rotterdam, Holland, 1949. Reprinted 1951.

Includes 'Marion Quinn'. A story in which Jack the Ripper teaches a young man to be his successor. The title of the book translates as 'Five Fantastic Stories'.

WRIGHT William	*Jack The Ripper Geht Um.* Aufwarts-Verlag, Munich, Germany, 1951

BECKER Benoit	*Le Chien Des Tenebres.* Fleuve Noir, Paris, France, 1955. Fleuve Noir, Paris, France, 1995.

FERNY Claude	*J'Etais Jack L'Eventreur.* Editions Metal, Paris, France, 1956. Editions Florent Massot, Paris, France, 1994.

Translates as 'I Am Jack The Ripper'.

REUBEL Theo	*Der Richter Von Whitechapel.* Liebel, Nurnberg, Germany, 1961.

McSHANE Mark	*Les Ecorches.* Gillimard, Paris, France, 1974, (Seire Noir No. 1665).

MOFFAT Gwen	*Jack The Ripper Brauchte Sechs.* Goldmann, Munich, Germany, 1975.

BOURS Jean Pierre   *Celui Qui Pourrissait.*
                                    Editions Marabout, Belgium, 1977.

SINIAC Pierre   *Aime Le Maudit.*
                                    Editions Jean Goujon, France, 1980.

NOLANE   *L'Heure De L'Eventreur.*
Richard D   Presses Du Crepuscule, Aix En
                                    Provence, France, 1980.
                                    (Limited to only 250 copies).

ELLIN Stanley   *Jack The Ripper Und Van Gogh.*
                                    Goldmann, Munich, Germany, 1980.
                                    Reprinted 1985 and 1989.

DUBOIS Pierre   *God Save The Crime.*
                                    Editions de la Brigandine, France, 1982.

REOUVEN Rene   *Elementaire Mon Cher Holmes.*
                                    Editions Deneol, Paris, France, 1982.

WAINWRIGHT   *D'Un Crime A L'Autre.*
John   Libraire Des Champs-Elysees, Paris,
                                    France,1982, (No. 1665).

PELLIER Evelyne   *Eldorado Et Cavaliers.*
                                    Maurice Nadeau, France, 1984.

                      **A novel which features Sherlock Holmes and Jack the
                      Ripper.**

HESSE Jerome   *Sir James.*
Olivier Orban, Paris, France, 1985.

A novel featuring Sir James Houseboard who is a sort of Sherlock Holmes character on the trail of Jack the Ripper who turns out to be Montague Druitt. Set in March 1889 this is well worth tracking down.

SHELDON S.K.   *Musee Des Horreurs.*
Gore Collection (No. 60), Fleve Noir, Paris, France, 1987.

A novel about a wax museum and Jack the Ripper.

SOJSHIMADA   *Hyakunen Ho Kadoku.*
Kirisaki Jakku   Shueisha, Tokyo, Japan, 1988.

A Japanese novel which features Jack the Ripper. Apparently translates as 'Jack the Ripper - 100 years of Solitude'.

VARATOJO Artur   *Na Pista De Jack O Estripador.*
Lisbon, Portugal, 1988.

A novel which features the Ripper, Sherlock Holmes and Doctor Watson.

BRAKMAN Willem   *Heer Op Kamer.*
Uitgeverij, Amsterdam, Netherlands, 1988.

A short story which takes place in and around Commercial Street at the end of the nineteenth century. Similar story to M. Belloc Lowndes' 'The Lodger'.

LIVINGSTONE J.B.	*Le Retour De Jack L'Eventreur.* Editions De Rocher, Monaco, France, 1989. Editions Gerard De Villiers, France, 1991.
DERSY Jean	*L'Horreur Est Humaine.* La Palindrome, Quebec, Canada, 1989.

Includes Jean Pettigrew - 'Pauvre Jack'. A short story.

SANTINI Gilles	*Eventrations.* Gore Collection (No. 116), Fleuve Noir, Paris, France, 1990.
REOUVEN Rene	*Les Grandes Profondeurs.* Editions Deneol, Paris, France, 1991. Reprinted 1994.

An excellent Ripper novel featuring also Robert Louis Stevenson and Oscar Wilde.

FREMIOT Pierre	*La Pompe A Biere Ne Repond Plus.* Editions Belfond, France, 1992.
HALTER Paul	*Rippero Manie.* Palace Noir, (No. 8), Bordeaux, France, 1992.
MENARD Emanuel	*La Derniere Victime.* Librairie des Champs-Elysees, Paris, France,1992, (No. 2084).

No Listed Author.   *So War Es! War Es So? Neue Unmogliche Interviews.*
                                        Wagenbach, Berlin, Germany, 1992.

                           **Originally published in Italy this book translates as 'Nine
                           Unimaginable Interviews'. Includes 'Jack the Ripper' by
                           Guido Ceronetti.**

SIRKIS   *La Grand Mere De Sherlock Holmes.*
Jean-Jacques   Seguier, Paris, France, 1995.

HALTER Paul   *Le Brouillard Rouge.*
                                        Editions Du Masque, France, 1996.

                           **An excellent Ripper short story contained in this
                           anthology of fiction.**

ODENE Laure   *Whitechapel.*
                                        Editions De Poche, Paris, France, 1997.

                           A novel where Jack the Ripper is born again.

LODI-RIBEIRO   *Outras Historias.*
Gerson   Editorial Caminho, Portugal, 1997.

                           **Includes the chapter 'Assessor Para Assuntes Furebres'
                           which contains references to Jack the Ripper. The chapter
                           translates as "Assistant on Funeral Matters'.**

Jack the Ripper
In New York
by
W.B. Lawson.
An early fictional work
published in 1891.

The Lodger
by
Mrs. Belloc Lowndes.
Longmans, New York, U.S.A.
1940 dustjacket.

Terror Over London
by
Gardner Fox U.S.A. 1957.
A rather scarce fictional account in paperback.

Jack the Ripper
by
Stuart James.
Monarch Books, U.S.A. 1960 paperback edition.

**Jack the Ripper
by Cherry Veheyne.**
This cover shows the
Australian paperback edition
published in Sydney.

**An Old Drama:
Three Encounters With
Jack the Ripper.
by Michael Gardner**
published in 1969.

**Susannah Beware
by T.E. Huff.**
This is the paperback edition
published in 1976 by Dell
Books. It was originally
released entitled "Nine Bucks
Row".

**Hands Of The Ripper
by Spencer Shew.**
Sphere Books, 1971,
paperback.

**The Return of
Jack the Ripper
by Mark Andrews.**
Leisure Books, U.S.A. 1977.

**Jill
by Thomas St. Martin.**
Dell Books, New York, U.S.A.
1979.

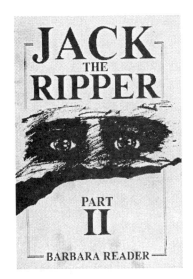

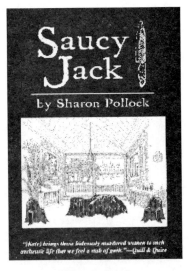

**Jack the Ripper Part II
by
Barbara Reader.**
1989 paperback.

**Saucy Jack
by
Sharon Pollock.**
1994 paperback. Canada.

**Sherlock Holmes Gegen Jack
the Ripper
by Ellery Queen.**
This is the 1968 German
paperback edition.

**De Wreker (The Lodger)
by
Mrs. Belloc Lowndes.**
This is an early Dutch edition of
this classic work.

**J'Etais Jack L'Eventreur
by Peter Marsch
(Claude Ferny).**
French 1956 paperback edition.

**Les Grandes Profondeurs
by
Rene Reouven.**
French 1991 paperback.

CHAPTER FIVE
A GUIDE TO THE MANY MAGAZINES
WHICH INCLUDE A FACTUAL ACCOUNT
OF THE JACK THE RIPPER MURDERS.

American Journal of Forensic Medicine and Pathology.
Raven Press Ltd., New York, USA.

Volume 2, Part 1. 1981.	William G. Eckert - *The Whitechapel Murders: The Case of Jack the Ripper*.
Volume 10, Part 2. 1989.	William G. Eckert - *The Ripper Project: Modern Science Solving Mysteries of History*.

Answers.
Amalgamated Press Ltd., London, UK.

2ⁿᵈ January 1943 – No. 2813.	Norman Colgan - *He Tracked Down Jack the Ripper*.

Antiquarian Book Monthly.
London. Countrywide Editions Ltd., Buckinghamshire.
January 1994. Volume 1,

Part 1, No. 237.	Brian Lake - *Jack the Ripper's Diary: Fake, Forgery, Spoof - or DoubleDetective Story?*
May 1999. Issue 296.	Richard Whittington-Egan - *Ripperature: The Books About Jack the Ripper*.

Armchair Detective (The).
White Bearlake Publishing, Minnesota, USA.
June 1976 Volume 9,

No. 3.	Albert Borowitz - *New Gaslight On Jack the Ripper*.

Beyond Magazine.

April 1931.	*Was Jack the Ripper A Spirit Obsession?*

Biblio. (Exploring The World Of Books).
(U.S.A.)
Aster Publishing Corporation, Oregon, USA.
August 1998. Volume 3,
No. 8.   Amy Hanson - *Bloody Fodder For The Pen:*
                          One Hundred and Ten Years of Jack The
                          Ripper In Print.

Bloodhound.
Burgho Press, London.
(Editor - Simon Wood).
March 1987. No. 1.   Contains a Jack the Ripper Article.
September 1987. No. 4.   Reviews Donald Rumbelow's
                          The Complete Jack the Ripper.

Book And Magazine Collector.
Diamond Publishing Ltd., London.
March 1993. No. 108.   Mike Stotter - A look at the many non-fiction works
                          that have been written about the infamous Murderer.
                          Includes bibliography and price guide.

Books And Bookmen.
London. 1965.   Richard Whittington-Egan - *Ghastly Murder.*
December 1972.   Colin Wilson - *The Duke And The Ripper.*

The British Medical Students Journal.
London. Autumn 1966.   Francis Camps - *Jack the Ripper.*

City.
(City of London Police Magazine)
February 1972.   B.E. Rielly - *Jack the Ripper: The Mystery Solved.*

Cloak and Dagger Club Newsletter.
London.
Issue 1 - Winter 1994/5.
Issue 2 - May 1995.
Issue 3 - September 1995. Produced in conjunction with the Cloak and Dagger
                          Club, for people with an interest in Jack the Ripper.
                          With Issue 4, changed it's name to 'Ripperologist'.
                          Edited by Mark Galloway.

Constabulary Gazette.
Ulster Journals Ltd., Belfast, Northern Ireland.
September 1983.   Peter Riley - *Jack the Ripper.*
November 1988.   Peter Riley - *A Century Of Jack the Ripper.*

Coronet.
Esquire Publishers, Chicago, USA.
November 1956.   Richard G. Hubler - *A Stunning Exploration of the Jack the Ripper Riddle.*

Cricketer (The).
London. January 1973.   Irving Rosenwater - *Jack the Ripper: Sort of a Cricket Person.*
December 1990.   Andrew Holloway - *Not Guilty.*

Crimes and Punishment Weekly.
Phoebus Publishing, London.
96 parts 1973 - 1975.
No. 17.   *Who Was Jack the Ripper?*
                                The Ripper's Reign of Terror.
No. 25.   *Scarlet Women.*
No. 46.   *Putting the Knife In.*

The Criminologist.
Barry Rose.   Law Periodicals, West Sussex, UK.
Winter 1968   Francis Camps - *More About Jack the Ripper.*
                                (This was also published in London Hospital Gazette No. 1. - April 1966).
Summer 1968   E.M. McLeod - *A Ripper Handwriting Analysis.*
Autumn 1971   Nigel Morland - *Jack the Ripper: A Final Word.*
Summer 1974   Donald Bell - *Jack the Ripper: Final Solution.*
Summer 1974   Derek Davis - *Jack the Ripper: A Handwriting Analysis.*
Spring 1988   John J. Dunne - *Jack the Ripper: A Century of Unremitting Mystery.*
Winter 1988   Joseph C. Rupp - *Was Francis Thompson Jack the Ripper?*
Summer 1988   Colin Kendell - *Did Mary Jane Kelly Die?*
Spring 1989   Colin Kendell - *Jack the Ripper, 1888 and All That.*
Spring 1989   Nicholas Warren - *A Postal Kidney.*

Spring 1990	Jay Mason - *Jack the Ripper: A Layman's Theory.*
Summer 1990	Colin Kendell - *The Intentions of T.E. Stowell.*
Autumn 1990	Roger Barber - *Did Jack the Ripper Commit Suicide?*
Spring 1991	John Southwell - *Bournemouth's Silent Man.*
Summer 1991	Garry Rowlands - *Shedding Some Light On The Ripper Letters.*
Spring 1992	Nicholas Warren - *Dr. Merchant Was Not Jack the Ripper.*
Winter 1992	Christopher Smith - *Jack the Ripper and The Alembic Connection.*
Spring 1993	William Henry - *The Ripper Case: New Evidence.*
Summer 1993	Christopher Smith - *An Exploration And Probe Into Motive.*
Summer 1993	Garry Rowlands - *Jack the Ripper: The Writing On The Wall.*
Autumn 1993	Christopher Smith - *The Millers Court Murder: Marie Jeanette Kelly: Victim or Accessory.*
Winter 1993	Nicholas Warren - *The Case Of Mr. Maybrick: Ripping Yarns.*
Winter 1994	Steve Fielding - *Was Jack the Ripper Hanged at Dundee Gaol?*
	Nick Warren - *Was James Maybrick The Victim Of An Untraceable Poison?*
Winter 1995	Stephen Wright - *Was Jack the Ripper An American?*
Summer 1996	Stephen Wright - A review of the Ripper bibliography '*Jack the Ripper*': *A Bibliography and Review of the Literature; by Alexander Kelly.*

Darkside (The).

Maxwell Specialist Magazines, London.

| July 1991. No. 10. | Jack the Ripper Special. |

Three chapters:

i) *Ripping Yarns* - Maitland McDonagh.
   Screen Career of Jack the Ripper.

ii) *Death's Deputy* - Stan Nicholls.

iii) Jack the Ripper And The World Of The Occult.

iii) *Butcher of Whitechapel.* - Allan Bryce.
   Examination of Facts of the Case.

Detective Cases.
August 1988   Thomas Conway - *Jack the Ripper: The Real Story.*

East London News: Jack the Ripper Edition.
Cullen Publications, Sydney, Australia.1988
                                A Centennial souvenir broadsheet with facsimile
                                reproductions of 1888 newspaper reports on the murders
                                with photographs of the murder sites.

Essex Ghosts And Hauntings.
Wesley Publications, Essex, UK.
No. 4. 1994.   *On The Trail Of Jack the Ripper:*
                                Was This Man Jack the Ripper?
                                (Article on William Gull).
No. 6. 1995.   *The Ghosts Of Jack the Ripper's Victims.*
                                By Wesley H. Downes.

Famous Crimes Past And Present.
London. 1903. Volume 2 The Story Of The Whitechapel Murders.
                                Edited by Harold Furniss.
Issue 15 - 16 - 17 - 18.   Reprinted 1998 by D. Froggatt, Birmingham.

Fate.
Clark Publishing Company, Chicago, USA.
May 1949. Volume 2,
No.1.   Hereward Carrington - *The Inside Story Of Jack
                                the Ripper.*

Highlander (The).
Barrington, Illinois, USA.
July/August 1992. No. 4.   Bryan Gordon - *Was Jack the Ripper A Scot?*

Historic Record (The).
John Wrigley, Sheffield.
January 1994. No. 30.   J.R. Wrigley - *Jack the Ripper Recorded.*

History Makers.
January 16th 1970.   J.S. Weiskopf - *Jack the Ripper.*

Horror Elite (The).
USA. April 1976. No.3.   Lyn Harkus - *The Harlot Slayer.*

Illustrated Police News Reprints.
Great Newspapers.   Published by Peter Way Ltd., London, UK.
Reprinted 1974   No. 25   *Jack the Ripper.*
                                     5 Newspapers in Colour Folder.
                                     i)   08 September 1888.
                                     ii)   22 September 1888.
                                     iii) 06 October 1888.
                                     iv)   20 October 1888.
                                     v)   17 November 1888.

In Britain.
Headway, Home and Law Publishing, London, UK.
June 1988.   Robin Mead - *Will The Real Jack (or Jill) Stand Up?*

Inside Detective.
Dell Publishing, New York, USA.
April 1977.   *Jack the Ripper Unmasked* by Ken Krippene.

International Crime Detective.
Independent Magazines Ltd., London, UK.
16ᵗʰ January 1977.   Ken Krippene - Exclusive - *Jack the Ripper*
No. 40.   *Unmasked.*

Journal Of The Society For Psychical Research.
Tavistock Square, London, UK.
(For Private Members and Associates Only).
July-August 1949.
Volume 35, No. 653.   D.J. West - *The Identity of Jack the Ripper:*
                                     An Examination of An Alleged Psychic Solution.

Life.
New York, USA.
13ᵗʰ November 1970.   P. O'Neil - *Parting Shots: Clarence the Ripper?*

Light.
London, UK.
(The Journal of College of Psychic Studies).
Autumn 1970.   Cynthia Leigh - *Jack the Ripper: A Look At The*
                                     R.J. Lees Theory.

Listener (The).
London, UK.
1st September 1988.
Volume 120, No. 3078.　　　　　John Triffitt - *Man Of Faction: The Jack the Ripper Myth.*

London Hospital Gazette (The).
Whitechapel, London, UK.
April 1966.　　　　　Francis Camps - *More About Jack the Ripper.*

Maryland St. Medical Journal.
Maryland, USA.
1979.Volume 28, No. 2.　　　　　B. Taylor - *Was Jack the Ripper Heir to the British Throne? - A New Book Says Yes.*

Master Detective.
Forum Press, London, UK.
September 1987.　　　　　Brian Marriner - *Murder And Magic.*
July 1993.　　　　　Michael Walker - *Did Jack the Ripper Murder In Bradford?*
Summer Special 1993.　　　　　Brian Marriner - *Was James Maybrick Jack the Ripper: Or Was His Diary A Hoax?*
　　　　　Dennis Parsons - *Jack the Ripper: The American Connection.*
　　　　　Dr. Forbes Winslow - *On The Streets of Whitechapel: Autumn 1888.*

Mean Streets.
What Goes On Pty., New South Wales, Australia.
August 1992. Issue 7.　　　　　Stephen Wright - *Jack the Ripper/Who Was Jack the Ripper?*
May 1994. Issue 11.　　　　　Stephen Wright - *The Diary of Jack the Ripper - Are They Real Or A Very Clever Fake?*

Men Only.
London, UK.
June 1973. Volume 38, No. 6.

　　　　　Daniel Farson - *Jack the Ripper: The Strange Obsession.*

Murder Casebook.
Marshall Cavendish, London, UK. 1991 Special Issue.

Who Was Jack the Ripper?
Contributor - Paul Begg.
Issued in Folder with free facsimile newspaper of the day, a reprint of the Illustrated Police News dated 06/10/1888.

Murder In Mind.
Marshall Cavendish, London, UK.

The Whitechapel Murders: Who Was Jack the Ripper?
Video special. 1997 Complimentary video enclosed entitled *The Whitechapel Murders.*
5 Chapters:
i)   *Outrage: First Blood.*
ii)   *More Victims: The Night of Two Killings.*
iii)   *Final Murder: The Horror at Millers Court.*
iv)   *Dead Ends: Chasing Shadows.*
v)   *Arrest: Closing In On The Ripper.*

Murder Most Foul.
Forum Press, London, UK.

July 1994. No. 13.   Mark Madden - *The Mystery of Mary Jane Kelly: Jack the Ripper's Last Victim.*

Oct. 1996. No. 22.   Jack the Ripper Special.
4 Articles:
i).Brian Marriner - *We Name Jack the Ripper.*
ii).A Contemporary Journalist - *Jack the Ripper: Six Chapters of Evil.*
iii).Matthew Spicer - *The Doomed Policeman Who Saw Jack the Ripper.*
iv).Bernard Brown - *Was Jack the Ripper A Policeman?*

Mysteries.
A Pirnell Magazine, MacDonald & Co. Ltd., London, UK.
First published 1978.
1988 Edition New and Updated.
Written and devised by Tim Healy -
includes - *Who Was Jack the Ripper?*

Mystery Scene.
USA.1994.No. 42.   John McCarty - *The Diary of Jack the Ripper: A
Conversation with Bob Miller the Hyperion Publisher.*

New Brunswick Reader (The).
New Brunswick Publishing Co., Canada.
31ˢᵗ October 1998. Volume 5, No. 48.
Daniel F. Johnson - *Jack the Quack: Did Jack the
Ripper Visit Saint John And Was It Here That He
Claimed His First Victim?*

New Family Researcher.
Old Tricon Press Ltd., London, UK.
April/May 1996.   *My Grandfather Knew Jack the Ripper.*
Freda Thomson interviewed by Marjorie McConnell Smith.

People Weekly.
Canada.
6ᵗʰ November 1995.   *Out Of The Past - Yankee Ripper: Was Jack,
London's Infamous Serial Killer, Really An American?*

Police Detective.
November 1985.   *Jack the Ripper - The Beast Who Walked By Night.*

Police History Society Journal.
Guildford, England, UK.
1990.No. 5.   Jon Ogan - *Martha Tabram: The Forgotten Ripper
Victim.*
1990.No. 10   Bernard Brown - *Was Jack the Ripper A Black
Magician?*

Police Review Magazine.
London, UK.

14TH August 1936.	Mervyn Millward - *The Terror Of The East End.*
	The Whitechapel Murders: Jack the Ripper.
	16 Articles 1977 - 1978 by William Vincent.
16th December 1977	*Slums of Shame.*
23rd December 1977	*Was Emma 1st Victim: Death Of An Unfortunate*
(Emma Smith).	
6th January 1978	*Slaying Of A Soldier's Sweetheart: Martha's Murder*
	More Than A Coincidence. (Martha Tabram).
13th January 1978	*Drunkard Joins The Death Trail. (Polly Nichols).*
	And A Detective Joins The Hunt. (Abberline).
20th January 1978	*Slit Throat And Abdomen Set Pattern. (Polly Nichols).*
	Witch Hunt Is On For Leather Apron Jack. (John
	Pizer).
27th January 1978	*Dark Annie. (Annie Chapman).*
	Death In A Pool Of Blood: Plot Thickens Amid Power
	Struggle.
3rd February 1978	*Strong Rap From The Coroner. (Bagster Phillips):*
	Suspects Arrested And Set Free.
10th February 1978	*Confessions Of A Cool Killer. (Dear Boss letter,*
	postcard)
	Or Letters From Expert Hoaxers?
24th February 1978	*Dutfields Yard Mystery (Liz Stride). The Missing*
	Hours To Murder.
3rd March 1978	*Second Murder Of A Night (Catharine Eddowes):*
	The Drunk Who Met Her Death.
10th March 1978	*Letters From The Ripper (From Hell) And The Writing*
	On The Wall (The Jews).
17th March 1978	*The Bloodiest Killing (Mary Kelly) And Then An*
	Illegal Cover Up or Lawful Withholding Of Facts.
24th March 1978	*Narrow Escape And Two More Killings (Mylett and*
	McKenzie). Suicide (Druitt), Suspicion, (Annie
	Farmer), and A Confession (W. Brodie).

31st March 1978	*An Anniversary Killing - The (Female) Torso Without A Name.*
4th April 1978	*The Last Killing (Frances Coles) And The Arrest Of A Bloodstained Seaman (Sadler).*
14th April 1978	*Suspects Line Up Now. Can You Pick Out The Ripper?*

Prediction.
London, UK. June 1973.

Joan Revill - *Read All About It: The 'Orrible 'Oroscope Of Jack the Ripper.*

Psychic Dimensions.
Charlton Publications, Connecticut, USA.
January 1975. Volume 2. No. 5.

Alex Findlay - *Who Was Jack the Ripper?*

Punch.
London, UK.
21st October 1987.

Tim Heald - *Rippering Yarns.*
(mainly book reviews).

Radio Times.
London, UK.
7th-13th July 1973.

Peter Gillman - *After the Ripper: My Knife Is So Nice And Sharp.*

Rave Reviews.
Mystery And Intrigue Magazine, USA.
1988

Richard Timothy Powyer - *The Crime Of The Century, The Mystery Of The Ages.*

Readers Digest.
London, UK and New York, USA.
June 1973 (USA Edition) July 1973 (UK Edition).

James Stewart Gordon - *The Enduring Mystery of Jack the Ripper.*

April 1983

Linda Gillard - *The Artist Who Painted Jack the Ripper.*

Real Crime Book Digest.
Presto Publishing, Chicago, USA.
Oct./Nov. 1993.
Volume 1, No. 4. Gary C. King - *The Alleged Diary Of Jack the Ripper.*

Real Life Crimes (And How They Were Solved).
Eagle Moss Publishers Ltd., London, UK.
1 No. 54.
Editors - Chris Bishop; Tricia Palmer and Ian Drury.

Jack the Ripper In Three Parts.
i) *Jack the Ripper: Whitechapel Murders.*
ii) *Did He Fall Or Was He Pushed?*
iii) *50 Yards Short Of The Perfect Murder.*

Writers - Peter Brookes-Smith; Chris Bishop and Patrick Tender.

Ripper Roundup.
A.J. Richards, Leicester, UK.
1996.Volume 2. Twenty six short articles on the crimes by enthusiasts, researchers and authors.
1995.Volume 1. Claimed to have been published with over fifty contributors. No copy can be traced.

Ripperana.
Greenford, Middlesex, UK. Quarterly magazine devoted to Jack the Ripper and other true crime cases. Founded 1992. Recommended. Edited by Nicholas Warren.

Ripperologist.
London, UK. Founded 1995, December. Issue 4. Magazine produced in conjunction with the Cloak and Dagger Club for people with an interest in Jack the Ripper. Six issues per year published on the first Saturday of February; April; June; August; October and December. Recommended. Edited by Paul Daniel.

Scandal.
Orbis Publishing, London, UK.
1990. Part 29. *Jack the Ripper Special.*
by Paul Begg.

Scots Magazine (The).
Dundee, Scotland, UK.
January 1988.   Euan MacPherson - *Jack the Ripper In Dundee.*

Sunday.
Free Magazine Issued With The News Of The World Newspaper, UK.
16ᵗʰ July 1995.   Anon - *Was This Jack the Ripper?*
                        Article which takes a look at suspect Dr. Francis
                        Tumblety discovered by Stewart Evans.

Sunday Express 3.
Free Magazine Issued With The Sunday Express Newspaper, UK.
14ᵗʰ September 1994.
                        Kenneth Baker - *Prince Of Scandal.*
                        A review of Theo Aronson's *'Prince Eddy and the
                        Homosexual Underworld'.*

Sydney Morning Herald Magazine.
Sydney, Australia.
5ᵗʰ November 1988   Daniel Farson - *Jack the Ripper: The Australian
                        Link*
                        Reprinted from *The Spectator* (London) (Date
                        Unknown).

The Damned Thing.
Hobgoblin Press, Bristol, R.I., USA.
Spring 1992. Volume 1. No. 2.
                        A Journal Of The Exotic And Bizarre.
                        Jack the Ripper Special. Edited by Sam Gafford.
                        Six Chapters (64 pages).
                        i)   *The Facts In The Case Of Jack the Ripper.*
                        ii)   *A Conspiracy Of Theories.*
                        iii) *Good Knight: An Examination Of The Final
                              Solution.*
                        iv)   *Red Ink - The Ripper In Literature.*
                        v)   *Ripping Films.*
                        vi)   *Reviews.*

Time.
Time Life International Ltd., Bradford.
29th August 1988.
Issue 35.   Helen Gibson - *In Britain: Jack the Ripper*
                                   Remembered.
9th November 1970.   Anon - *Who Was Jack the Ripper?*

Time Out.
London, UK.
24th-31st August 1988.
No. 940.   Christopher Frayling - *Ripping Yarns.*

Tit Bits.
London, UK.
12th May 1962.   Normal Inglis - *Was Jack the Ripper Caught?*

True Crime Monthly.
Forum Press, London, UK.
April 1982.   Bruce Paley - *A New Theory On The Jack the*
                                   Ripper Murders.

True Crime (Summer Special).
Forum Press, London, UK.
July 1999.   John Ogan and Nick Connell – *A Trip Down*
                                   Blood Alley.

True Detective Magazine.
Forum Press, London, UK.
January 1973.   Leonard Gribble - *Was Jack the Ripper a*
                                   Black Magician?
                                   Reissued in January 1988 edition.
March 1977   Leonard Gribble - *The Man They Thought Was*
                                   Jack the Ripper.
November 1987   Nicholas Warren - *99 Years And Still The World's*
                                   Greatest Mystery: Jack the Ripper.
December 1987   Griffith S. Salway - *I Knew Jack the Ripper.*
                                   Taken from March 1949 USA edition.
December 1987   Klas Lithner - *Elizabeth Stride: Swedish Ripper*
                                   Victim.
December 1988   Brian Marriner - *Looking Back On Jack the*
                                   Ripper.
January 1989   Brian Marriner - *Enigma Of George Chapman.*

| November 1993 | Bruce Paley - *We Name Jack the Ripper.* |
| November 1993 | Mark Madden - *Jack the Ripper: The Irish Connection.* |

Trusty Servant.
December 1972. No. 34.	James Sabben-Clare - *Jack the Ripper.*

Two Worlds.
London, UK.
21ˢᵗ February 1959.	Anon - *Medium Solved Britain's Vilest Murders. (The Lees Story)*

Umpire.
Manchester, UK.
31ˢᵗ July 1910.	Anon - *Who Was Jack the Ripper?*

Unexplained (The): Mysteries of Mind, Space And Time.
Orbis Publishing, London, UK.
1983.No. 65.	*The Murders And The Medium.*
1983.No. 132	*At Home With the Ripper*
1983.No. 133	*Was the Ripper Part Of A Plot That Involved The Masons And Royalty.*

Uri Geller's Encounters Magazine.
The World's Most Paranormal Magazine.
Paragon Publishing Ltd., Dorset, UK.
January 1997. Issue 3.	Gavin Baddley - *In The Shadow Of The Ripper.*

W.A.D.E. Journal.
Chicago, USA.
June 1975. Volume 2.
No. 1.	Thomas J. Mann - *The Ripper And The Poet: A Comparison In Handwriting.*

Weekend Book Of Murder And Mayhem.
Harmsworth Publications Ltd for Associated Newspapers Group, London, UK.
1983.	Edited by Tony Wilmot.
	Richard Whittington-Egan - *The Riddle Of The Vanishing.* (Ripper cover also.)

Whitechapel Journal.
New York, USA.
Founded Fall 1996.   Published twice a year - Fall and Spring.
                                           Edited by Stephen Wright.
                                           Mostly Book Reviews.

Who Was Jack the Ripper?
Pipeline Publication, Surrey, UK.
1988.   One-off publication.
                                           By Winston Forbes Jones.

Women's Realm (The).
London, UK.
11th October 1988.   Sarah Craske - *Who Was Jack the Ripper?*

World Atlas.
USA.
Autumn 1977. Volume 1.
No. 3.   Timothy J. Rutt - *The Stalker In The Dark:*
                                           Jack the Ripper And World Newton.

XS.
Free Magazine Issued With The Sunday Mail Newspaper, Glasgow, UK.
8th June 1997.   Noreen Barr - *Was This Man The Real Jack the*
                                           Ripper?
                                           A review of Jim Tully's book *The Secret of*
                                           Prisoner 1167 - Was This Man Jack the Ripper?
                                           And a look at his suspect James Kelly.

FACTUAL ARTICLES CONTAINED
IN FOREIGN LANGUAGE PUBLICATIONS.

Alter Ego.
Spectra Communications, Quebec, Canada.
June/July 1994.　　　　　　　Christian R. Page - *Sincerement Votre Jack*
　　　　　　　　　　　　　　L'Eventreur.
　　　　　　　　　　　　　　Written in French.

Atomovision.
French Fanzine.
1996 No. 4.　　　　　　　　*Jack L'Eventreur.*

Bzzlletin.
The Hague, Holland.
Literair Magazine.
No. 206/207. Volume 22.
May/June 1993.　　　　　　*Nora Oomen Capteyn - Your Own True Loving Friend:*
　　　　　　　　　　　　　　Jack the Ripper Als Literair Personage.

Charlie.
Paris, France. No. 4.　　　　Willem - *Chez Les Misogynes.*

Cold Sweat.
French Fanzine.
1988. No. 3.　　　　　　　　*Jack L'Eventreur.*

De Groene Amsterdammer.
Amsterdam, Holland.
19th October 1988.　　　　　Frans Van Hout - *Jack the Ripper: Een Sportieve*
　　　　　　　　　　　　　　Britse Cricketspeler.
12th January 1993.　　　　　Martin Van Amerongen - *Jack the Ripper: Ik Geloof*
　　　　　　　　　　　　　　Dat Ik Stapelkrantzinning ben: Buurman Moordennar.
　　　　　　　　　　　　　　An article which looks at the many suspects including
　　　　　　　　　　　　　　Ostrog and Kosminski.

Dicosexe.
Paris, France.　　　　　　　Jean Pierre Bouyoux - *J'Comme Jack*
No. 4.　　　　　　　　　　*L'Eventreur.*

Dossier Meurte.
A.L.P. Publications, Paris, France.
1991. No. 2.   *Jack L'Eventreur.*

Gang.
No. 1.   Jean Claude Asfour - *Le Boucher de Whitechapel.*

Histoire Pour Tous.
Paris, France.
No. 84.   R. Derlome - *Jack L'Eventreur, L'Homme Qui Fit
                                       Trembler L'Angleterre.*

Historama.
Paris, France.
No. 252.   Tom Cullen - *Qui Etait Jack L"Eventreur.*

Historia.
Paris, France.
No. 201.   L. Treich - *L'Enigme de Jack L'Eventreur.*
No. 302.   L. Blatin - *Une Altesse Royale, Jack L'Eventreur.*
No. 367.   G.M. Tracy - *Du Nouveau Sur Jack L'Eventreur.*

Intermediair.
Dutch Magazine.
26th November 1993.
Volume 29. Issue 47.   Anon - *Einde Van Het Raadsel?*
                                       An article which looks at James Maybrick.

Jury.
Stockholm, Sweden.
1973. No. 2.   Klas Lithner - *Vem Var Jack Uppskararen?*
                                       (Who Was Jack the Ripper?)

Knack.
N.V. VTU Publishers, Brussels, Belgium.
31st August 1988.   Rik Van Cauwelaert - *Moord als Moderne Kunst.*
                                       An article which looks at Jack the Ripper and
                                       Scotland Yard.
15th February 1995.   Geert Lernout - *Een Sublieme Leugen.*
                                       Contains references to Jack the Ripper.

Le Cri Du Lycanthrope.
Strasbourg, France.
April 1983. Fanzine.
No. 1.   Manuel Hirtz - *Dossier Jack L'Eventreur.*

Le Figaro.
Paris, France.
August 1988. No. 20 - 21.   Vincent Gerard - *Jack L'Eventreur.*

L'Histoire.
Paris, France.
December 1983. No. 62.   Roland Marx - *L'Enigme Jack L'Eventreur.*

Miroir De L'Histoire.
Paris, France.
No. 186.   G.M. Tracy - *Jack L'Eventreur.*

Monster Bis.
Paris, France.
Fanzine. No. 11.   *Jack L'Eventreur.*

Mysteres.
Paris, France.
January 1994. No. 7.   Fabien Bleuze - *Jack the Ripper - Le Tueur Aux Mille Visages.*

New Look.
Paris, France.
November 1993. No. 124.   Stephane Bourgoin - *Le Journal De Jack L'Eventreur.*
                                Discusses the Diary and Shirley Harrison's book.

Veronica-Gids.
Dutch Magazine.
18th-24th November 1989.   Hette Visser - *Wie Was Jack the Ripper.*
Issue 46.

Vrij Nederland.
Dutch Magazine.
18th September 1993.   *Geen Mes In Jack the Ripper.*

CHAPTER SIX.
A GUIDE TO THE MANY MAGAZINES WHICH INCLUDE A FICTIONAL ACCOUNT OF THE JACK THE RIPPER MURDERS.

Absurd.
Ian Caunce, Rochdale, Lancs, UK.
September 1988. No. 4.

> Jack the Ripper Special. Amateur fanzine detailing films and television shows featuring the Ripper.

All Hallows.
The Ghost Story Society Magazine.
October 1998. No. 19.

> Includes the Ripper Short Stories;
> i). C.E. Ward - *End Of The Line.*
> ii). Simon MacCulloch - *Fog.*

Argosy.
Richard Kyle Publication, California, USA.
August 1991. Volume 3. No. 3.   Ellery Queen - *A Study In Terror Part I.*
December 1991. Volume 3. No.4.   Ellery Queen - *A Study In Terror Part II.*

Armchair Detective.
White Bear Lake Publishing, Minnesota, U.S.A.
1978. Volume 8. No. 3.   Eileen Snyder - *Was Watson Jack the Ripper?*

Baker Street Christmas Annual.
London, UK.
1960   Thomas Grady - *Two Bits From Boston.*

Baker Street Journal.
London, UK.
January 1949. Volume 4.
No. 1.
December 1965.
Volume 15. No. 4

December 1967.
Volume 17. No. 4.
December 1967.
Volume 17. No. 4.
June 1968. Volume 18.
No. 2.
June 1968. Volume 18.
No. 2.
June 1968. Volume 18.
No. 2.
Sept. 1968. Volume 18.
No. 3.
June 1978. Volume 28.
No. 2.

Page Helenbrand - *Another Bohemian Scandal.*
Flemming Christensen - *Who's Afraid Of Big Bad Jack: Or An Attempt To Disclose The Identity Of Jack the Ripper.*

Bruce Kennedy - *Jack In The Abyss.*

Bruce Dettman - *Who Wasn't Jack the Ripper?*

Flemming Christensen - *Who Wasn't Turner?*

Edward S. Lauterbach - *Holmes And The Ripper.*

Alex N. Salowich - *He Could Not Have Sat Idly.*

Jack Leanitt - *Mr. Holmes Please Take The Strand.*

Ninetieth Anniversary Jack the Ripper Memorial Issue.
Andrew S. Hannah - *The Most Tragic Case: Sherlock Holmes And Jack the Ripper.*
David J. Kiser - *The Curious Incident of The Whitechapel Murders.*
John M. Linsenmeyer - *The Editors Gas-Lamp.*
Harold E. Niver - *Mr. Sleuth - Holmes or Moriarty?*
R.A. Faguet - *I am A Doctor Now Ha Ha.*
Julia Rosenblatt & - *The Elizabeth Stride Memorial*
Fredric H. Sonnenschmidt *Kidney Recipes.*

Bloodhound Detective Story Magazine.
T.V. Boardman & Co., London, UK.
January 1962. Volume 1.
No. 9.

Richard Ellington - *The Ripper.*

Canadian Holmes.
Toronto, Ontario, Canada.
Magazine of Bootmakers of Toronto.
Autumn 1988. Volume 12.
No. 1.   Jack the Ripper Special.

Castle of Frankenstein.
Gothic Castle Publishing, New York, USA.
1972. Volume 5. No. 3.

Includes reviews of the two Hammer films 'Hands
of the Ripper' and 'Dr. Jekyll and Sister Hyde' by
Calvin T. Beck.

Ellery Queen's Mystery Magazine.
Davis Publishing, New York, USA.
August 1972.   Anthony Boucher - *A Kind Of Madness.*
August 1972.   R.L. Stevens - *The Legacy.*
March 1976.   Robert Bloch - *A Most Unusual Murder.*
October 1978.   Edward D. Hoch - *The Treasure Of
                             Jack the Ripper.*
May 1945.   H.H. Holmes -*The Stripper.*

Fangoria.
O'Quinn Publishers, New York, USA.
January 1986. No. 50. John Wooley - *Savini the Ripper.*
                             A look at the 1985 made for video film 'The Ripper'
                             starring Tom Savini.

Fantastic Adventures.
Ziff Davis Publications, New York, USA.
July 1946. Volume 8.
No. 3.   David Wright O'Brien - *The Softly Silken Wallet.*
                             A pickpocket picks a wallet from a musician and
                             finds that it has the happy quality of producing
                             money, but the money is bloodstained and the wallet
                             has a strange feel. The musician is a Jack the Ripper
                             type killer who makes wallets out of human skin.
Fate.
Chicago, USA.
October 1995.   Andy Ellis - *Jack's Back.*

Fear.
Shropshire, Newsfield Publication.
Fantasy and Science Fiction, Horror Magazine.
Jan/Feb. 1989. No. 4.   Kim Newman - *Many Unhappy Returns.*
     Part I of a Ripper Filmography.
March/April 1989. No. 5.   Kim Newman - *Pieces Of Hate.*
     Part II of a Ripper Filmography.
May 1990. No. 17.   Peter T. Garratt - *Legions Of The Night. (Short Story).*

Filmfax.
Filmfax, Illinois, USA.
February/March 1992.
No. 31.   Gary Colville & - *Jack the Ripper: His Life And* Patrick Lucanio - *Crimes In Popular Entertainment.*

Guilty Detective Story Magazine.
Feature Publications, New York, USA.
July 1957. Volume 2.
No. 1.   W. Shannda - *Worse Than Jack the Ripper.*

Hitchcock Magazine.
H.S.D. Publications, New York, USA.
July/August 1991. No. 30.   Robert Arthur - *Said Jack the Ripper.*
     Originally published December 1957.

The Listener.
London, UK.
16th December 1965.   L.W. Bailey - *The Case Of The Unmentioned Case. (Sherlock Holmes As Jack the Ripper).*

Magazine Of Fantasy And Science Fiction.
Mercury Press, Connecticut, USA.
1951.   Kay Rogers - *Love Story - A Tale of Jack the Ripper.*
1991. August. Volume 81, No. 2.
     David Hoing – *City Of The Dreadful Night.*

Magazine of Horror.
Health Knowledge Publications, New York, USA.
April 1965.   Reynold Junker - *Jack.*

Manhunt.
Flying Eagle Publications, New York, USA.
February 1963. Volume 11. No. 1.

Jack Ritchie -*Ripper Moon.*

Masque.
Leicester, England, UK. May 1971. No. 14.

Film magazine which devoted this issue to Sherlock
Holmes, Jack the Ripper and 'gaslight' films.

Midnight Shambler.
David Barker, Salem, USA.
February 1988. No. 1.

R. Chandler - *Ripper's Nightmare.*

Mike Shayne Mystery Magazine.
Renown Publications, New York, USA.
October 1980. Volume 44.
No. 10.

Sweet Violets by Michael Avallone.

This story sees the Ripper disguise himself in human
form when actually he is a monstrous non-human
creature.

Million.
London, UK.
The Magazine of Popular Fiction.
March/June 1993.
No. 14.

Kim Newman - *Forever On The Prowl.*

The many appearances of Jack the Ripper in
fiction and film are catalogued.

Mystery.
USA. September 1981.
Volume 3. No. 2.

Tim Kelly - *Jack On Stage: Those Ripping Plays.*

Mystery Lovers/Readers Newsletter.
USA. July 1973.
Volume 6. No. 1.

Edmund J. Nolan - *Jack Of Many Trades: Some
Uses Of The Ripper On Screen.*

Necronomicon.
Andrew Black, Devon, UK.
February 1994.   No. 4.   *A Study In Terror* is reviewed as well as *Hands of the Ripper* by Tim Greaves; and the 1976 film *Jack the Ripper* starring Klaus Kinski is discussed by Andrew Stroud.

Pontine Dossier.
Luther Norris, California, USA. 1974.
                                Raymond Jones - *Jack the Ripper: Some Ruminations On The Whitechapel Fiend.*

Primetime Magazine.
Wider Access Television Publication, London, UK.
1989.   No. 15.   Kim Newman - *Jack On The Box.*

Queen Magazine.
London, UK.
September 1970.   Graham Norton - *Was Gladstone Jack the Ripper?*

Saint Detective Magazine (The).
King Size Publications, New York, USA.
September 1962.
Volume 8. No. 7.   Edward D. Hoch - *The Ripper Of Storyville.*

Samhain.
John Gullidge, Devon, UK.
Aug/Sept. 1988. Issue 10.   Andrew Black - *Ripping Yarns: A Study Into The Scarlet Terror Of Saucy Jack - An Enigma Of Our Crime.*

Scarlet Street.
Scarlet Street Publications, New Jersey, USA.
Summer 1995.   No. 19.   i.)   Richard Valley - *A Study In Terror.*
                                ii)   Lelia Loban - *New Masks For Jack the Ripper.*
                                iii) Richard Valley - *Sherlock Holmes Meets Ellery Queen.*
                                iv)   Jessie Lilley - *Herman Cohen On How To Make A Monster Movie.*

The Sherlock Holmes Detective Magazine.
Berkshire, UK.
1997 Issue 21.   David Stuart Davies - *Holmes Of The Movies:*
                                   A Study In Terror.

Shivers.
Visual Imagination Publications, New York and London.
The Magazine of Horror Entertainment.
May 1995. No. 18.   Mark Gratiss - *Just For Jolly: The Life And*
                                   Crimes of Jack the Ripper.
                                   A look at the films and television shows which
                                   feature The Ripper.

Short Stories Magazine.
October 1958. No. 1.   John Morresey - *To The Memory Of The Dead.*

Showtime.
USA. December 1965.   Anon - *No Wonder They Call Him Jack the*
                                   Ripper.
                                   A short story which apparently also features
                                   Sherlock Holmes.

Terror Australis.
Leigh Blackmore, Sydney, Australia.
The Australian Horror and Fantasy Magazine.
Summer 1992. Volume 2.
No. 3.   Jack the Ripper Special.
                                   (Edited by Leigh Blackmore).
                                   Fanzine type publication which looks at short
                                   stories books, records, comics, verse etc. on
                                   the Ripper.

The Tombstone Epitaph.
Arizona, USA.
May 1997. No. 5.   Ben T. Traywick - *The Demise Of Jack the*
                                   Ripper.

Video Watchdog.
T & D Lucas, Ohio, USA.
Jan/Feb. 1993. No. 15.   Gregory Mank - *Hollywood's Reluctant Ripper.*

Videotopsie
D. Didelot, Viriat, France.
November 1997.   No. 7.   Jack the Ripper Special.
Edited by David Didelot.
French Fanzine discussing films, television shows
and books produced, all on the subject of the
Ripper.

Week End Novels.
Allied Newspapers, Manchester, UK.
The following nine issues contained a serialised
short story entitled *The Whitechapel Mystery:
A Story Of Nameless Terror.*
Issue No. 573 - 15th November 1930.
Issue No. 574 - 22nd November 1930.
Issue No. 575 - 29th November 1930.
Issue No. 576 - 6th December 1930.
Issue No. 577 - 13th December 1930.
Issue No. 578 - 20th December 1930.
Issue No. 579 - 27th December 1930.
Issue No. 580 - 3rd January 1931.
Issue No. 581 - 10th January 1931.

Weird Tales.
Short Stories Inc., New York, USA.
July 1943.   Robert Bloch - *Yours Truly Jack the Ripper.*

World Of Horror.
Dallruth Publishing Group, London, UK.
Circa 1970's.   No. 3.   Includes *The Jack the Ripper Musical.*

CHAPTER SEVEN
COMICS AND GRAPHIC NOVELS.

2000 AD.
Mandarin, London.
Special, 1992.   *Killing Time* by John Smith and Chris Weston.

2000 AD.
Egmont Fleetway Ltd., London.
25th Feb/10th Mar. 1998.   *Cruel Britannia* by Robbie Morrison and
                                   Simon Fraser.
                                   Comic Strip which includes eleven Jack the
                                   Ripper type characters.

2000 AD.
Fleetway Publications, London.
15th June 1991.   *Ripping Yarns* includes Killing Time by John
                                   Smith and Chris Weston. Published weekly
                                   continuing the story thereafter. Issues 735 - 744.

Amazing Heroes.
Fantagraphics.
1st October 1985. No. 80.   *Down For The Count And Ripped To Shreds.*
                                   Ed Sample interviews Rickey Shanklin and Mark
                                   Wheatly. Features previously unpublished
                                   illustrations.

Asylum.
Millennium Publications, Narragansett, USA.
No. 2. (Not dated, circa 1990's) features;
                                   The Knife Of Jack the Ripper.
                                   Writer -   Marv Channing.
                                   Illustrator -   Vicente Alcazar.
                                   Colourist -   Paul Davis.

Bad Girls Blackout.
Blackout Comics Inc. New Jersey, USA
1995 No. 1. By Guy Dorian. *Lady Vampre.*
Written by John Platt.
Created by Bruce Schoengood.
Jack the Ripper pits his wits against a vampire.

Baker Street - Children Of The Night.
Caliber Comics, Tome Press, Plymouth, Missouri, USA.
1993 Issues 1 - 5. By Guy Davis and Gary Reed.
Contains much Ripper content.

Blood Of The Innocent.
Warp Graphics, New York, USA.
Drawn and written by Rickey Shanklin, Mark Wheatly and Marc Hempel.
Four Issue Mini Series 1986.
7th Jan. Issue 1. Includes *Two Victorian Gentlemen* by Robert Bloch.
14th Jan. Issue 2. Includes *Dracula Bram Stoker's Bogeyman* by Rickey Shanklin.
21st Jan. Issue 3. Includes *The Life And Deaths of Jack the Ripper* by Rickey Shanklin.
28th Jan. Issue 4. Includes *Whitechapel: The Shame Of London* by Rickey Shanklin

Classic Judge Dredd.
Fleetway Editions Ltd., London.
September 1996. No. 14. *Night Of The Ripper!*
Judge Dredd versus Jack the Ripper.

Comics Journal (The).
N.B.M. Publishing, New York, USA.
December 1994. No. 173. *Messages From Hell: From Hell- Book One, The Complete Scripts.* A review by Rich Kreiner.
May 1994. No. 168. *Victoria's Secret: From Hell. Vol. 1- 4.* A review by Edward Shannon.

Creepy.
Warren Publishing Co., New York, USA.
October 1968. No. 23. *Jack Knifed.*
Story by Bill Parente.
Artwork by Barry Rockwell.

October 1981. No. 125.   *His Own Private Demon.*
Story by Roger McKenzie.
Artwork by Anton Caravana.
Features Montague Druitt.

Doom Patrol (The).
D.C. Comics, New York, USA.
June 1989. No. 23.   *The Butterfly Collector* by Grant Morrison.
July 1989. No. 24.   *The House That Jack Built* by Grant Morrison.

Dracula Lives.
Marvel Comics Group.
October 1973. No. 3.   *The Vampire Man.*
Features vampires, a hunchback, Scotland Yard
and, of course, Jack the Ripper.

Eternals Annual (The).
Marvel Comics Group.
October 1977. No. 1.   *The Time Killers.*
Story and Artwork by Jack Kirby.
The Ripper makes an appearance in a story
involving the godlike Eternals and time-travel.

Frankenstein.
USA Comic.
1975. No. 1.   G. Kane - *Jack the Ripper.*

From Hell.
Mad Love Publishing, Mass. USA.
Written by Allan Moore.   Illustrated by Eddie Campbell.
Ten separate volumes issued between 1991 -
1998.

Wonderful publication of a re-working of the
Stephen Knight theory. Issues were rather
sporadically published. Recommended.

From Hell.
Mad Love Publishing, Mass, USA.
Subtitle - Dance Of The Gull Catchers.
September 1998. Volume 11.

An epilogue to the award winning Jack the Ripper saga detailed above, by Allan Moore and Eddie Campbell.

Gotham By Gaslight.
D.C. Comics, New York, USA.
1989.

An Alternative History Of The Batman.
Script by Brian Augustyn includes 'From Hell' by Robert Bloch introduction.
Gotham City in 1889 with The Ripper on the loose tracked by Batman.

Hair Raisers.
Longman, Essex, USA.
1981 Part Two.

Jack the Ripper.
Written by -   Cliff Edwards.
Illustrated by -   Michael Strand.

A comic book aimed at children which tells the story of The Ripper. Part of a four issue series.
Others include:
Part One - Sweeney Todd.
Part Three - Burke and Hare.
Part Four - Dr. Jekyll and Mr. Hyde.

House Of Mystery (The).
D.C. Comics, New York, USA.
July 1980. No. 282. Volume 30.

Fear runs rampant as a modern day Jack the Ripper stalks the City and is stalked, in turn, by a vampire.

July 1982. No. 306.
Volume 32.

I Vampire.
Jack the Ripper is on the loose again in London.

Jack The Ripper.
Caliber Comics, Tome Press, Plymouth, Missouri, USA.
April 1999.   Writer -   Gary Reed.
                                     Illustrator -   Mark Bloodworth.
                                     A comic which includes a detailed factual study
                                     of the case. A must for collectors of factual Ripper
                                     material also.

Jack The Ripper.
Eternity Comics, California, USA.
Three Issue Mini Series.   Written by Bruce Balfour.
                                     Artwork by Paul Mendoza.
                                     Issue 1 - October 1989.
                                     Issue 2 - January 1990.
                                     Issue 3 - February 1990.
                                     Based on Stephen Knight's *Jack the Ripper: The
                                     Final Solution.*

Jack The Ripper.
Malibu Graphics Inc., California, USA.
September 1990.   Written by Bruce Balfour. Issues 1, 2, and 3 of
                                     the Eternity Comics publications, grouped
                                     together and published in book form. (New Front
                                     Cover).

Jacquelyn The Ripper.
Eros Comics, Seattle, USA.
August 1994   A modern day female version of Jack the Ripper
                                     features in this strictly adults only publication.

Journey Into Mystery.
Marvel Comics Group.
December 1972. 2nd Series.
No. 2.   *Yours Truly Jack the Ripper.*
                                     Story by Ron Goulart and Roy Thomas.
                                     Adaptation of the Robert Bloch tale.

Masters Of Terror.
Marvel Comics Group.
July 1975. No. 1.

A reprint of the *Journey Into Mystery* comic (Dec. 1972) featuring Robert Bloch's *Yours Truly Jack the Ripper.* This issue contains a short biography of Bloch.

Maze Agency (The).
Comico Publishers, USA.
March 1989. No. 4.

The Return Of Jack the Ripper by Mike Barr. The murder victim in this story is a member of a modern day Ripperologists Club!

Night's Children.
Millennium Comics, USA.
1995 No. 1 & No. 2.

Ripper.
Includes Jack the Ripper content by Wendy Snow-Lang.

Predator Nemesis.
Dark Horse Comics, Oregon, USA.
December 1997. No. 1.
January 1998.   No.2.

Writer - Gordon Rennie.
Artist - Colin MacNeil.
Two part story featuring The Ripper.

Psycho Killers M.I.A. Special.
Zone Publication Comics, New Jersey, USA.
December 1992. Volume 1.
No. 2.

Jack the Ripper.
Mike Obre & Dan O'Connor.

Pulse Of Darkness.
Opal Press, Australia.

0)   Volume 1. No. 2.   *Silent Murder.*
Story by C. Sequeira. Artwork by Kurt Stone. Detective Rattlebone trails Jack the Slasher making fun of Stephen Knight and Alfred Hitchcock's 'The Lodger'.

Scarlet In Gaslight.
Eternity Comics, California, USA.
Four Issue Mini Series.   No. 1. - December 1987.

No. 2. - January 1988.

No. 3. - February 1988.

No. 4. - March 1988.

Story by Martin Powell and Wayne R. Smith.
Artwork by Seppo Makinen.
Makes clear that The Ripper was a cross between
Professor Moriarty and Count Dracula. Also
published in complete form by Eternity Comics in
1989.

Sherlock Holmes In The Case Of The Missing Martian.
Eternity Comics, California, USA.
Four Issue Mini Series.   No. 1. - June 1990.

No. 2. - July 1990.

No. 3. - August 1990.

No. 4. - September 1990.

Story by Doug Murray. Artwork by Topper
Helmers.
Involves a sub plot where Doctor Watson's wife is
suspected of being Jack the Ripper.

Spring-Hell Jack: Revenge Of The Ripper.
Rebel Studios, California, USA. 1993.

By David Barbour and Wayne Tanaka.
A special three issue series devoted to both Spring
Heeled Jack and Jack the Ripper.

Taboo.
Spiderbaby Grafix and Publications, Vermont, USA.
1989 Nos. 2 - 17 include serialisation *From Hell*

Written by Allan Moore.
Illustrated by Eddie Campbell.

Treasury Of Victoria Murder (A).
N.B.M. Publishers, New York, USA.
1995   *Jack the Ripper.*

Written and Illustrated by Rick Geary.
An excellent adaptation of the Whitechapel
Murders in hardback/book form.

Vamperotica Annual.
Brainstorm Comics, USA.
1995 No. 1.   Jack the Ripper content.

Vampire Tales.
Marvel Comics Group.
February 1975. Volume 1.
No. 9.   *The Bleeding Time.*
                               Story by Gerry and Carla Conway.
                               Tale influenced by Robert Bloch's 'A Toy For
                               Juliette'.

Warp Graphics Annual.
Warp Graphics, New York, USA.
January 1986. No. 1.   *Christmas Spirits.*
                               Story by Rickey Shanklin and Mark Wheatly.
                               An epilogue to 'Blood Of The Innocent' (Jan.
                               1986).

Wonder Woman Amazonia.
D.C. Comics, New York, USA.
1997   William Messner-Loebs, Paul Winslade and
                               Patricia Mulvihill are responsible for this graphic
                               novel which features The Ripper.

Young Witches (The).
Eros Graphic Annuals, Seattle, USA.
June 1997. Book 2.   *London Babylon.*
                               By Solano Lopez and Barreiro.

                               A graphic annual featuring Jack the Ripper and
                               Dr. Jekyll and Mr. Hyde. Aimed at adults only due
                               to it's highly explicit nature and extreme
                               pornography.

COMICS AND GRAPHIC NOVELS.
FOREIGN LANGUAGE.

Batman: Jack The Ripper Er Tilbage.
Denmark. Comic.
1991 No. 16.   Danish edition of *'Gotham By Gaslight'*.

Cauchemar.
France. Comic.
1972. No. 6.   *Jack L'Eventreur.*

Fantomen.
Sweden.   By Idi Kharelli.
                                A comic book which sees London terrorised by
                                the Ripper who is none other than Donald
                                Rumbelow! The comic is illustrated in
                                Rumbelow's 1987 revised hardback.

Jack - Les Adventures De Basil Et Victoria.
Les Humaneides Associes, Geneva.
1992.   One-off publication by Edith and Yann.
                                A 51 page graphic novel/annual in full colour in
                                which two children, Basil and Victoria, find
                                themselves in London 1888.

Jack L'Eventreur En Vacances.
Editions Du Square, Paris, France.
Et Beacoup D'Autres Histoires by Willem
Published 25th February 1974.
                                French comic book which takes a light-hearted
                                view of the Jack the Ripper murders.

Jack The Ripper/Ortiz-Segura.
1st published 1991 - Dalger Press, Barcelona, Spain.
Also   1992 - Loempia, Netherlands.
                                Black and white comic book charting the
                                Ripper murders.

Le Crime Ne Pays Pas.
France-Soir, France.
1953 No. 1.   R. De Valerio - *Jack L'Eventreur*

Sherlock Holmes.
Le Franq, Brussels, Belgium.
January 1994. No. 29. *Jack L'Eventreur.*
Hardback graphic novel on the crimes, consisting of 48 pages in full colour. Published as part of the 'Le Masque Detective' series. Also published as: *Jack the Ripper.*
As above except in paperback. as part of the 'Collectie Detective Series'.

Spirou.
France. Comic.
1982 No. 2308. Bercovici, Yamm and Conrad.
Jack L'Eventreur.

Terror.
Elvifrance, France. Comic.
1971 No. 6. *La Veritable Histoire De Jack L'Etrangleur.*

Terror.
Tilburg, Belgium.
No Date. No. 18. *Jack the Ripper Special.*
Black and white pulp comic book.

Thriller.
Editions Campus, France.
Circa 1980's. No. 7. Alain Pauchard.
Sherlock Holmes Contre Georges L'Egorgeur.

Tintin.
France. Comic.
1981. No. 28. M. Scheter and Y. Duval.
Jack L'Eventreur.

U-Comix.
Germany.
Comic-Straps Fur Erwachsene.
Circa 1980's. Volume 10. Issue 112.
Contains *Jack the Ripper* by Tilo Rothacker.

CHAPTER EIGHT.
COLLECTABLES.

As we have seen Jack the Ripper has featured in a vast amount of books, comics and magazines over the years, however it does not stop there. Collectors and enthusiasts have a plethora of other items to whet their appetites. This section takes a look at the ephemeral and associated collectables produced, all featuring Jack the Ripper.

Jack's London Map.
A unique 1880's map with period drawings which take you into the dark world of fog, gaslamps, alehouses, prostitution and murder in Jack the Ripper's London. Produced by Daryl Sullivan and Andrew Cockell and published by Geonex, London in 1994.

Jack the Ripper's Occult Plan.
For the five Whitechapel Murders. Friday 31st August - Friday 9th November 1888. A detailed map showing the murder sites of the canonical five, using sacred or secret geometry. Designed and produced by Ivor J. Edwards, Surrey, 1998.

Jack the Ripper's London.
A map covering Whitechapel, Spitalfields etc., showing places of importance e.g. Ten Bells Public House; Goulston Street Graffitti site. Taken from an 1893 Ordnance Survey map. Produced and printed by R & P Hinton, Wales in 1998. A laminated version measuring 24" x 17" and an unlaminated version measuring 33" x 24" are available.

Jack the Ripper Walk: Louis' London Walks.
A small detailed booklet published by Louis' London Walks in 1998 designed to enable the reader to conduct their own tour of the major Ripper sites and buildings connected to the case. Nicely produced.

Autumn of Fear Information Cards.
A set of 36 cards giving information regarding the suspects, victims etc., all involved in the Jack the Ripper case. Designed by Karl Derrick, Deborah Hyde and Floyd Jones-Hughes, they were published by Fanta Co., Albany, New York, USA in 1993.

Mystery Rummy Card Game.

Case No. 1 - Jack the Ripper.

A card game for two to four players where the object of the game is to try to unmask the Ripper. The game includes 25 gavel cards, 36 evidence cards, 1 Ripper escapes card and a rule booklet. It was created by Mike Fitzgerald and released in 1998 by US Games Systems, Stamford, USA.

A nice item.

Three Letters From Hell: Letters Reputedly In The Hand Of The Whitechapel Murderer.

This ephemeral item was published by the Lands End Press, USA, in 1988. It is a small volume which contains facsimiles of the *Dear Boss, I Was Not Codding* and the *George Lusk Letter*. Of the 175 copies which were published, 100 were presented to the members of the Zamorano and Roxburghe Clubs at their September 1988 joint meeting. They were presented by Wade C. Hughan, the proprietor of the Lands End Press.

Jack the Ripper Trading Card.

Published as part of the True Crime Trading Card Set released by Eclipse Enterprises Inc., California, USA in 1992. The card states that the Ripper's identity was never discovered.

Jack the Ripper Computer Game.

Released by Spectrum in 1987. It was distributed by Electronic Arts with an '18' certificate. Can only be played on what is now obsolete equipment.

Ripper Computer Game.

A CD-Rom computer game designed by Dennis Johnson. Distributed by Take 2 Interactive Softward Inc., USA, 1995.

Jack the Ripper Computer Game.

A CD-Rom computer game issued by Gametek, Florida, USA in 1995. The game invites you to solve the mystery. The full box set includes CD's, a user's manual and an attractive Ripper poster.

Jack the Ripper Board Game.
The mystery game of the Whitechapel Murders of 1888. It was first produced in America in 1983 by Sleuth Publications Inc., of San Francisco and proved so poular that it was again released in 1985 and 1986. The game itself is very complicated and needs serious concentration, which undoubtedly takes away some of the fun, which is the real reason for playing the game in the first instance. A game for only two players, one will take the role of Police Commissioner, Sir Charles Warren, and the other, naturally, plays Jack. Playing the killer is the more difficult part and the instructions manual advises the more experienced player to assume this role. Included in the game are an eight page rule book (which needs to be referred to constantly), a mounted map of Whitechapel, 40 advantage cards, a status sheet, 88 playing pieces, a six sided dice and 10 suspect cards who are named as Prince Albert Victor, JK Stephen, Sir William Gull, Walter Sickert, Montague Druitt, a medical student, a foreign sea captain, a cab driver, a police constable and Leather Apron, aka John Pizer. The object of the game is for one player (Warren) to save London from the scourge of Jack the Ripper. He will try to use his Constables, Sergeants and Inspectors to thwart the killer. The player can also receive help from Scotland Yard or hire a Private Investigator to eliminate suspects until he successfully unmasks 'The Monster of Whitechapel'.
Collectors will find the game difficult to obtain, especially in Britain, however there is an enthusiast devising his own board game which he hopes to market in the near future.

Jack the Ripper Clock.
Produced in 1988 the clock shows an illustration of the Ripper lurking in Commercial Street. This is a hard to find item.

Zippo Lighter.
Produced in 1998 to accompany publication of John Smithkey III's book 'Jack the Ripper': The Inquest Of The Final Victim Mary Kelly'. The face of the lighter shows the dustjacket used on the book . A nice collectable.

Jack the Ripper Fishing Lure.
This unusual item was produced by Red River Fishing Lures of Louisiana, USA in the 1990's.

Jack the Ripper Model Figures.
A small amount of figures or models have been released over the years showing the killer. Available in metal, lead and plastic.

Pub Signs.
A wide selection of Pub signs, in a variety of sizes, featuring Jack the Ripper, are available.

The London Dungeon.
The London Dungeon which of course houses the famous 'Jack the Ripper Experience' has, over the years, been responsible for a number of Ripper collectables and ephemeral items. The Ripper has featured on T-Shirts, coffee mugs, thimbles, pens, pencils, keyrings, fridge magnets, beer mats, postcards, bookmarks and bar towels to name but a few. Tourists to the Dungeon snap up these niknacks which remind them of their visit to London and the 'Jack the Ripper Experience.

Jack the Ripper Coin/Token.
Produced in America, this item was part of the Honouring History Series and showed the Ripper with a knife in his hand. Released in 1976 it was also called a 'Devil Dubloon'.

Jack the Ripper Belt Buckle.
This is available in America and made from pewter. A rather nice item.

Theatre Programmes.
A large number of plays based on the Whitechapel Murders have been staged, both professional and amateur, worldwide and the advertising posters and handbills as well as the programmes are nice mementos and excellent collectables, especially the early productions.

Film Material.
Many films have been based on or around the Whitechapel Murders, some have been excellent productions others not so good. There is a wealth of related material to interest the collector. Film posters, front of house stills, lobby cards, press books, original film scripts etc.are all worth owning. Of course these items do not come cheap especially anything associated with Hammer who made three Ripper films - i. Hands Of The Ripper; ii. Dr. Jekyll and Sister Hyde; iii. Room To Let.

CHAPTER NINE.
AUDIO TAPES.

The World's Greatest Mysteries.
A boxed cassette which looks at famous mysteries. As well as 'Who Was Jack the Ripper?' it includes 'The Abominable Snowman' and 'The Bermuda Triangle' plus many others. Published by Hamlyn Books on Tape, London 1988.

Martin Fido.
Ripper author and historian, Martin Fido, has released three separate audio tapes detailing the Jack the Ripper murders:

i.) On the Trail of Jack the Ripper - An investigation into the trust identity of the most famous and elusive murderer of all time.
> Released by LBC Bookpoint in 1992.
> Produced by Paul Savory.

ii). In The Footsteps of Jack the Ripper - Released by the Talking Tour Company this cassette also contained a map of Whitechapel. 1994.

iii). True Crime - Jack the Ripper - Published by MCI with Speaking Tours Ltd., as part of the Crime and Thriller Collection. Issued in 1995.

Arthur Douglas - Will The Real Jack The Ripper.
Audio cassette version of the book published in 1979 by the Countryside Press
(2 x 45 mins). Read by William Maxwell.

The Diary Of Jack The Ripper.
Released on audio cassette and read by Nicholas Ball.

Tony Strafford - The True Story Of Jack The Ripper.
A double CD released by The Stow Music Company in 1997 detailing all the facts surrounding the Ripper case. Not available in cassette form.

CHAPTER TEN.
Music And Recordings
Featuring Jack the Ripper.

A Study In Terror Soundtrack.
Published by South Mountain Record, BMI, England.
Released by Roulette Records, 1966.

Jack the Ripper (1958) Soundtrack.
Released by RCA Victor and RCA Camden 1959 and 1960.
Dialogue from the move soundtrack.
The complete story of the world's most wanted criminal.
Incidental music by Stanley Black. With narration by Cedric Hardwicke.
Music composed by Jimmy McHugh and Pete Rugolo.
Album produced by Neely Plumb.

Hammer Presents Dracula With Christopher Lee.
EMI Records 1974. Music composed by James Bernard.
Side two, track 4, - Dr. Jekyll and Sister Hyde.

Blood! The Life And Future Times Of Jack The Ripper.
Alternate World Recordings, 1977, 2 x LP set.
Robert Bloch reads 'Yours Truly Jack the Ripper' and 'A Toy For Juliette'. Harlan
Ellison reads 'The Prowler In The City At The Edge Of The World'.

The Ballad Of Jack The Ripper And Other Cockney Songs.
Southern Music, London, 1974. Album.

Time After Time Soundtrack.
Album. Entracte Label, 1979. Music composed by Miklos Rozsa.
Produced By John Steven Lasker and Nicholas Meyer. Also available on CD.

Die Musik Zum Musical Jack The Ripper.
Quality Entertainment Productions, Hamburg, Germany.
1994 A seventeen track CD produced by Timo Blunck. All of the songs sung in German.

Yours Truly Jack The Ripper.
A musical concept by Frogg Moody. Narrative written by David Taylor and read by
Colin Burden. A ten track CD. Wiltshire, 1998. Recommended.

Alice Cooper - Raise Your Fist And Yell.
An album released by MCA Records, London, in 1987.
It contained the song 'Chop, Chop, Chop' sung by Alice Cooper and Kate Roberts and related to Jack the Ripper.

Tampa Red - Jack The Ripper Blues.
A recording made in Chicago, USA, in 1931 by Tampa Red, real name Hudson Whittaker, and released on the Vocation label.

Black Widow - Black Widow.
An album which contained the Ripper related track Mary Clarke.   The music was published by April Music/Magus Music CBS.

Screaming Lord Sutch And The Savages.
Released a single entitled 'Jack the Ripper' in March 1963 on the Decca label (No. F.11598). Released a record entitled 'Hands Of The Ripper' in 1972.
The UK edition was on Atlantic (No. K 40313) 1973, and the American issue was on Cotillion (No. 9049). This version was re-issued as 'Jack the Ripper' in August 1987 on the Konnexion label (Koma 788018). A version of this track also appeared on Sutch's 'Rock And Horror' CD released by Ace Records (No. CDCHM65) in 1992.

Judas Priest.
Released a track entitled 'Ripper' on the album 'Sad Wings From Destiny' in 1975.

Thin Lizzy.
Released a song based on Jack the Ripper entitled 'Killer On The Loose' in 1980.

Link Ray And His Ray Men.
Released a song entitled 'Jack the Ripper' on Ace Records in 1963 (No. CH 6).   The song also featured on the album 'Stuck In Gear' released by Virgin Records in 1976, (side 2 track 4).   It again featured on an album called 'It's Only A Movie' by the band who were now known as The Raybeats.   The album was released by Unit 7 Records in 1983, and again in 1984.

The Milkshakes.
Contributed their version of the Link Ray song 'Jack the Ripper' to an album entitled 20 Great Guitar Instrumentals released by Cascade Records circa 1983.

One Way Streets.
Their compilation 'Back From The Grave' featured a song entitled 'Jack the Ripper'. Released in 1986, it can be found on Volume 1.

L.L. Cool J.
Released a 12 inch record on Def Jam Recordings (CBS) which contained the song 'Jack the Ripper'. The song was written by Rick Rubin and J.T. Smith (real name of L.L. Cool J) and was released in 1988.

The Fuzztones.
Released a record on the Northern Songs label in 1989 entitled 'Jack the Ripper'. It was a B-side and was produced by Shel Talmy.

Morrissey.
The ex lead singer of the group 'The Smiths' released a song 'Jack the Ripper' in 1992 on 'His Master's Voice' label. It was produced by Mick Ronson and engineered by Peter Jones.

Nick Cave And The Bad Seeds.
Released 'Jack the Ripper' in 1992 on Mute Records, England.
It was written by Nick Cave and produced by David Briggs, Mick Harvey and Nick Cave.

The Jeff Newell Quartet.
Released an album in 1999 entitled JACK THE RIPPER although, apart from the title, it has nothing at all to do with the Ripper. This jazz recording was released on Igmod Records (No. 49806).

Hits Of The Sixties.
An album released by Polydor in 1966 which contained a track entitled 'Jack the Ripper'. (No. 236527A).

Univers Zero.
A French group who released a single entitled 'Jack the Ripper' (no date). It was written by D. Denis and R. Trigaux.

Reg Owen And His Orchestra.
Released an album entitled Manhattan Spiritual which contained the track 'Jack the Ripper' written by Fred Weismantel. It was available on the Pye International label.

The Surfaris Play.
Included the Song 'Jack the Ripper' (by Fred Weismatel) on an album released by Brunswick, England in 1963.

Carlos Malcolm And His Afro-Jamaican Rhythms.
Released an album entitled 'Rukumbine'. Side 2, track 1 was 'Jack the Ripper' written by Carlos Malcolm.

Stinky Toys.
A French punk rock band included the track 'Jack the Ripper' on their album 'Stinky Toys' released by French Polydor in 1997 Words and music by Elli Medeiros and D. Jacno.

Chris Turner Band.
A pub band from Sydney, Australia are reputed to have recorded a song about Jack the Ripper which remains unreleased. Exact date of recording unknown.

Surprise.
Released an L.P. entitled 'Reformation' which contained the track 'Jack the Ripper'. It was released on U.S. label Refuge Records. Words and music by Alexander MacDonald.

Toys Went Berserk.
Released an album entitled 'The Smiler With The Knife' in 1990 on Aberrant Records. The band originated in Sydney, Australia. No direct connection to The Ripper but the title is suggestive of Jack.

Nino Tempo With Pete Rugolo And His Orchestra.
Released the single (45 rpm) 'Jack the Ripper' on RCA Victor (No. 477694) in the USA. No date is given

Monster Mash: Sounds Of Terror For Halloween.
(The Scary Fun Record). Pickwick Internations Inc., USA, 1974.
This record contains a track entitled Jack the Ripper, plus others including The Mummy's Revenge and The Curse Of The Zombies.

CHAPTER ELEVEN.
USEFUL INFORMATION.

Ripperana Magazine.
Published quarterly this is a must for anyone interested in Jack the Ripper. This true crime mystery magazine devotes the vast majority of it's pages to the Ripper case. Recommended.
Available from: Nick Warren (Editor),
16 Costons Avenue,
Greenford,
Middlesex,
England, UB6 8RJ.

Ripperologist Magazine.
Published six times per year, this magazine is the official magazine of the Cloak and Dagger Club who meet every two months in London to discuss the Ripper case. The magazine itself is devoted to all aspects of the Jack the Ripper mystery and is, once again, a must for all Ripper enthusiasts. A yearly subscription also includes free membership of the Club. Recommended.
More details from:
Paul Daniel (Editor),
66 Shaftesbury Avenue,
London,
England, W1V 7DF.

Whitechapel Journal.
Published twice per year this is more of a newsletter than a magazine, it mostly contains book reviews; but does seem to be expanding it's factual articles.
Available from: Stephen Wright,
PO Box 1341,
F.D.R. Station,
New York,
NY10150-1341,
USA.

Ripper Notes.
The Quarterly Newsletter of Casebook Productions Inc.,
Editor - Sam Gifford; Co-Editor - Chris George;
Assistant Editor - Jon Smyth.
A quarterly magazine devoted to the Ripper mystery which was first published
in May 1999. Recommended.
Enquiries to: Chris George,
                Casebook Publications Inc.,
                3800 Canterbury Road,
                Apt. 3E,
                Baltimore,
                MD 21218, USA.

TRUE CRIME BOOKDEALERS WHO SPECIALISE IN JACK THE RIPPER.

Ross Strachan Books,
66 Cairn View,
Galston,
Ayrshire,
Scotland, UK,
KA4 8LY.

Regular lists of new and out of print Jack the Ripper books, magazines etc.
Also conducts a free Jack the Ripper Booksearch. Wants lists welcome.

Grey House Books, (Camille Wolff),
47 Kersley Street,
Battersea,
London,
England.
SW11 4PR.

Issue regular true crime catalogues which contain a substantial section
devoted to Jack the Ripper.

Loretta Lay Books,
24 Grampian Gardens,
London,
England,
NW2 1JG.

Issue regular true crime catalogues and specialise in Jack the Ripper material.

Les Bolland,
9 Birch Close,
Broom,
Bedfordshire,
England,
SG18 9NR.

Issues regular true crime catalogues which also contain a large Ripper
section.
Booksearches undertaken.

Clifford Elmer Books,
8 Balmoral Avenue,
Cheadle Hulme,
Cheadle,
Cheshire,
England,
SK8 5EQ.

Issues regular true crime catalogues which contain occasional Ripper
sections.
Wants lists welcome.

Janus Books,
PO Box 40787,
Tucson,
Arizona,
AZ 85717,
USA.

Booksellers who issue catalogues which contain small Ripper sections.

Mordida Books,
PO Box 79322,
Houston,
Texas, 77279.
USA.

Issue catalogues with occasional Ripper titles.

Geoffrey Cates Books,
1268 Cedar Street,
Oshawa,
Ontario,
Canada,
L1J 3S2.

Issues catalogues of true crime books and specialises also in Jack the
Ripper material.   Wants lists welcome.

Rupert Books,
58-59 Stonefield,
Bar Hill,
Cambridge,
England,
CB3 8TE.

Bookdealers who specialise in Sherlock Holmes and Arthur Conan Doyle
literature who also carry a small stock on Jack the Ripper.

THE RIPPEROLOGICAL PRESERVATION SOCIETY.

PO Box 9232,
Paramus,
New Jersey,
NJ 07653,
USA.

Reprints contemporary and early works related to the Ripper case.

THE LONDON DUNGEON.

28-34 Tooley Street,
London,
England,
SE1 2SZ.

A museum of horror which houses the 'Jack the Ripper Experience'.

INTERNET.

A recommended site on the internet is:

http://www.casebook.org/

ABOUT THE AUTHOR.

Ross Strachan is twenty nine years old, married and lives in Ayrshire, Scotland. He has been interested in the Jack the Ripper mystery for eleven years. He is an avid collector and has amassed a huge amount of books and ephemera relating to the case. He has also appeared on television with part of his collection.

Other interests include Hammer Films; actors Peter Cushing and Tod Slaughter; and sport – especially football. He is a lifelong supporter of Kilmarnock Football Club and has followed them all over Europe and beyond.